More Aspects of Spalding

in words and photographs by Michael J. Elsden

Front cover picture: the River Welland from a painting.

Dedication

To my grandson Zak William Elsden.
That he will appreciate our heritage.

Author:
Michael J. Elsden

Published by:
Bookmark
The Crescent, Spalding.

Produced by:
Elsam Cross & Co.
Printers
London Road, Spalding.

ISBN: 0953958213

0953958221 (Special Edition)

Printed in England.

2001

Contents

Acknowledgements

Without the help of quite a few people it would be very difficult to produce a book like this. Many people have come forward with photographs, and information which has been invaluable, for which I am grateful.

I wish to thank the Council of the Spalding Gentlemen's Society for allowing me access to the archives, and giving me permission to reproduce some of the Hilkiah Burgess watercolour paintings of the town.

Mr. Tom Royce has been very helpful in checking my text about the railways, and for allowing me to copy some of the photographs from his collection for which I thank him. Thanks are also due to Mr. Redhead and Mr. Trevor Bell for supplying me with some of the photographs.

Finally I must thank Christine Hanson of Bookmark for publishing my work, and my wife and family who all give me much continued support.

MICHAEL J. ELSDEN

Publishers Request

Many people reading this book will have stories of their own to tell and photographs that would be of great interest to other readers. Would you like to share them and help us record our history for future generations?

We invite you to help us publish *Aspects of Fenland People*, *Aspects of the Fens in Photographs to 1945* and *Aspects of the Fens in Photographs 1945-2000*.

If you think you can help please write, telephone of visit us at Bookmark, 20 The Crescent, Spalding, Lincs. PE11 1AF. Telephone 01775 769231.

We look forward to hearing from you.

Thank you for your continued support.

Christine Hanson

Bookmark, Spalding

Introduction

At the beginning of the 19th century Spalding had a far smaller population than today, nevertheless the town was a busy bustling place. The river traffic was in full swing, as this was before the railways had been built. At this time the river was navigable inland to beyond Stamford, and provided a good service for transporting coal, agricultural produce, and all kinds of heavy goods to places along its course. The inhabitants of Spalding often took their exercise walking along the riverside from High Bridge to the Pigeon Inn on the Holbeach Road. When the river was busy there would have been much of interest to see, especially at high tide when the air would be coloured with the language of the sailors.

The tides in the Welland brought up the river shoals of Butts. Butts were the local name for Dabs which are small Plaice. These were gathered on the slips after the water receded providing those that collected them with a free meal. The fishermen used Butt Pricks – a stick with a sharp nail at the end for gathering them. They were slippery, and gathering them by hand would be too slow.

The area around the Pigeon Inn was populated by sailors and their families, and was quite a flourishing quarter. Some of the gentry built their houses beside the river closer to the town, and close by were the warehouses that provided storage for the wares that passed through the port. There were many public houses both sides of the river as well as throughout the town providing a meeting place for recreation and doing business.

Shopping in the 1800s was far different to today. The grocer only sold groceries, he would not dream of stocking bread, flour, hardware or fresh fruit, and the baker only sold flour, bread and cakes etc. The butcher was where you bought your meat, and he would not sell other shopkeepers wares. There were no compulsory holidays in those times, but if you were lucky your employer would let you have Good Friday and Christmas Day off, but not every shopkeeper was as generous. The closing of the shop at night had to wait until the departure of the last customer, usually a woman, who often showed complete disregard for the comfort of the shop staff. On Saturdays the shops would be open until eleven or later, and the delivery of goods often had to be done on the Sabbath.

In the early 1800s the health and hygiene in the town was very poor. Sanitation was almost non-existent, and those who lived alongside the river often disposed of their effluent in its waters. The poor of the town lived under terrible conditions, and tuberculosis was common among younger women. This was not helped by the fact that the water supply was unfit for human consumption. Where people had their own wells the water was usually contaminated. The water-carriers delivered water around the town. It was taken from the River Glenn and the Vernatts Drain. This water was a little more tolerable, but it had to be paid for, so the poor did not use it.

Spalding enjoyed fame for its theatricals. Plays were performed in the Assembly Rooms that stood where the Spalding Club now stands in Broad Street. At regular intervals a travelling company spent a season in a tent in the yard of the Pied Calf Inn in Sheep Market. This company would give a different play every night for a week which would include Shakespearean tragedies, comedies, old English plays, and modern dramas.

The practice and the enjoyment of music was the monopoly of a small majority of the inhabitants. Not many of the population would own a piano, and Spalding in the 1800s was said to be deficient in really good solo singers, particularly of tenors. This was said to be due to the Fenland air, which was thought in those days to not be favourable to the production of singing voices. By the middle of the 19th century music became a little more popular due to a substantial impetus from the enthusiasm of Mr. and Mrs. C. R. C. Proctor, of

London Road, and Mrs. Tongue mother of Mrs. Proctor. These talented artists promoted the practice of orchestral and chamber music. Local instrumentalists rallied to them, and were encouraged to practice hard. Mrs. Proctor's orchestra became a popular institution.

As the 19th century came to a close there had been much improvement made in the standard of living. The river trade had diminished as the railway spread throughout the country. In the middle of the century a new Corn Exchange was built providing more opportunity for entertainment. In the field of public health great strides were made. A water company had been founded, who provided piped water around the town, and a modern hospital was built due to the generosity of two sisters, Elizabeth Ann Johnson and Mary Ann Johnson.

In the following pages can be experienced a look into what Spalding was like in the years gone by. As to what has improved, and what is not as good the reader is left to judge.

Business Trade & Profession

The Bulb and Flower Industry

The bulb and flower industry around Spalding started in the 1880s, but it is uncertain who the first person was that started growing and marketing bulbs. In the early days the three major players were: J. T. White, Oscar D'Alcorn and R. D. Wellband, but the first person mentioned in the Lincolnshire Directories was Mrs Elizabeth Quincey who is listed in 1885 as a Bulb Merchant and Wholesale Fruiter.

The first growers specialised in snowdrops, daffodils and narcissus. Some of the snowdrops were sold for medicinal purposes, but it was J. T. White who first sent cut flowers to the market at Covent Garden.

In 1907 Samuel Culpin, who had been in the bulb industry since 1897, planted the first Darwin Tulips in the Spalding area. These varieties which had long stems followed after the cropping of daffodils, giving both a good cut flower, and also a crop of bulbs.

The forcing of flowers under glass started in 1920 and rapidly expanded as more people entered the growing industry. In the 1930s an annual flower show was held in the Corn Exchange, which gave growers a chance to see and buy new varieties of bulbs. Spalding growers placed a large quantity of Lincolnshire grown bulbs on the market, and buyers found these were as good as the bulbs that had previously been obtained from Holland.

In the period leading up to the Second World War the Hawthorn Bank Nurseries of H. M. Bates provided a wonderful show during the Spring months, when acres of beautiful tulips, daffodils and hyacinths were ready for the market.

Another extensive bulb farm was that of Elsom's who started growing in Spalding in 1891. Messrs. Elsom's specialised in early double-tulips for forcing and bedding.

Many acres of bulbs were cultivated by Stassen Limited, a firm which was conducted in conjunction with J. Stassen, Junior, of Hillegom, Holland who set up nurseries in Pinchbeck Road, Spalding in order to market British-grown bulbs, and employ British workers.

With the onset of the Second World War restrictions were placed on the growing of bulbs as the land was needed for an increase in food production. Food rationing remained until 1953, but once this was lifted the bulb industry expanded rapidly, and by 1958 there was about 6000 acres of bulbs being grown in the area. It was also in 1958 that the annual Tulip Parade was started in Spalding, followed in April 1966 with the opening of Springfields Gardens at Fulney on the outskirts of the town. These gardens were built as a shop window for the British bulb industry, and for many years attracted visitors from far and wide.

The 1970s saw the bulb industry reach its peak in production, and since then there has been a steady decline in the production of tulips. On the other hand the production of daffodils is expanding, and it is said that we now produce more than the Dutch. As to the future of the bulb industry only time will reveal, but it is certain that there is nowhere near as many growers as there used to be.

Advert from 1933.

The cropping of narcissus at Spalding. Early 1900s.

The cropping of narcissus at Spalding. Early 1900s.
Notice the special wheelbarrow for carrying the flowers.

Wheeling his barrow full of flower boxes is Mr. David Waldock (father of the late Bert Waldock) at his nursery and greenhouses in St. Johns Road, Spalding. The lady in the black dress bunching and packing the flowers is thought to be his wife. Photograph taken in the 1920s.

The site of where David Waldock's nursery once stood. Photographed here in 1998.

David Waldock also farmed land between Bourne Road and Pennygate, and here can be seen workers cropping. What the crop is is not clear, but it is known that he grew radishes in these fields.

A field of tulips in bloom on the Bulb Farm of H. W. White, Cradge Bank Nurseries, Spalding.
In the background making the scene very picturesque is Rhodes Mill. The sails were taken off in 1939, and the upper part of the mill taken down in 1943, leaving the stump which still remains.

Advert from 1950.

Advert from 1937.

Bulb Growers in Spalding in 1937.

Bailey, Jn. Wm., Spalding Common.
Barnard, Wilfred, Fulney Bridge.
Barnett, Thos., Stonegate.
Bateman, P. (Miss), Lower Fulney.
Bates, Helen M. (Mrs), Hawthorn Bank.
Baxter, B. & Son, Park Road.
Bland, Cyril, "Riomar", Low Road.
Castle, Stanley, 33 Cowbit Road.
Clarke, Albert, Matmore Gate.
Cook, Bristo, Horseshoe Road.
Croxford, Jn. A., Fulney Lane.
Culpin Bros, Narcissus Gardens.
Culpin Sidney, The Chestnuts, Low Road.
Dalcorn Frederick, 283 Pennygate.
Drury, J. J. & Son, Little London.
Elsom, George, Elsom House, Broad Street.
Everett Bros, 30 Queens Road.
Ford, Jn. Wm., Deeping High Bank.
Fountain, Arth., Spalding Common.
Goodrum, Arth., Melton, Little London.
Gostelow Jn. S., The Hollies, Fulney.
Groom Bros. Ltd., Pecks Drove.
Hadden Wltr. Leslie., Low Fulney.
Hanson Chas. Wm., 2 Claylake Road.
Harpham J. & Sons, Willow Walk.
Harpham Hy. Rd., Low Road.
Harris Edward, Childers Drove.
Healey, H. & Sons, 112 Winsover Road.
Hill, R. A. B., Regent Nurseries.
Jacob, Edward Wm., St. Thomas's Road.
Killingworth Chas., Claylake Road.
Kitching Bros., The Cedars, Queens Road.
Lincoln Nurseries Ltd., Cradge Bank.
Merryweather Tom, 109, London Road.
Monks House Bulb Co. Ltd., Bourne Road.
Nell Bros., Wygate Road.

Parkinson, Ronald, Pennygate.
Plumb, Thos. & Jn., Cowbit Road.
Rodwell, Thos. B., Fulney Farm, Lower Fulney.
Rogers, Phillip, Clay Lake.
Rowlatt, Jn. Rt., The Green, Hawthorn Bank.
Seymour Cobley Ltd., Spalding Marsh.
Simmons, D. & R., Park Road.
Slooten, Cornelius, Cowbit Road.
Sly, Harold Frederick, Holbeach Road.
Smith, Stanley H. B., Inglewood, Holbeach Road.
Spalding Bulb Co. Ltd., Horseshoe Road.
Stagles, J. & Son, Fernleigh, Pennygate.
Waldock, Wm. Herbert, Shipley House, Bourne Road.
Wellband Rd, Dawson, 78 London Road.
White, J. T. & Sons Ltd., Little London.
White Henry W., Cradge Bank.

Advert from the
Lincolnshire County
Handbook of 1935.

H. Leverton & Co. Ltd.

Herbert Leverton started in business as a cycle dealer in High Street, Spalding about the year 1900. Besides cycles Herbert also traded in farm machinery, and equipment, but his main interests were soon channelled towards the motor car that was just beginning to make its appearance on the streets of our towns. It was in 1901 that he bought his first car, which he found to be rather unreliable. Experience was soon gained into the mechanics and workings of the car with his "do it yourself" repairs. Word soon got around as to his abilities in car repairs, and within a short time he was able to find enough work to employ him full time in car maintenance.

In 1904 Mr. F. Myers injected some money into Leverton's business, and went into partnership with him. By 1907 they were able to open a motor garage in High Street.

On the 30th June, 1909 the partnership acquired the former Drill Hall premises in Sheep Market, and the business began to prosper, with the increase in popularity of motoring. Shortly after this Herbert Leverton went on a world cruise, but he never completed the tour as he died a few years later in Hobart, Tasmania.

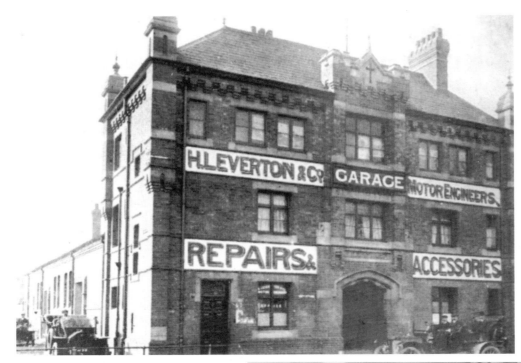

H. Leverton & Co.'s garage in Sheep Market. This building was formerly the Drill Hall.

View of the interior of Leverton's car showroom on 12th October 1909 when 24 cars were accommodated. Inset are Fred Myers, left, and H. Leverton, the proprietors of the business.

Leverton's main factory in Westlode Street. About 1970.

Leverton's car showroom in Pinchbeck Road on the right. About 1968. The Pinchbeck Road factory was on the left opposite the showroom.

Leverton's garage for motor repairs in Broad Street. This closed down in the early 1970s.

Leverton's Tractor showroom in Westlode Street.

Scene outside Leverton's Pinchbeck Road depot.

During the 1914-18 war Mr. Myers was appointed controller of agricultural tractors in Holland County which led to the need for additional premises for the expanding business. Despite doubts from local farmers, Caterpillar tractors gradually took over from the old steam engine drawn ploughs.

After the war demand increased for tractors, and Leverton's business continued to grow. In 1935 H. Leverton & Co. Ltd., were appointed as Caterpillar dealers alongside Jack Oldings. Leverton's covered the North of England, from the Scottish border to a line from Liverpool to Harwich. Oldings covered Southern England and Wales. In 1950 Jack Olding relinquished his dealership and Leverton's Spalding depot became responsible for country wide Caterpillar Service.

Up to this time Leverton's still kept an interest in the motor car trade, holding dealerships for Jaguar, Rover and Austin cars. The garage in Broad Street was responsible for the service and maintenance of cars. In the early 1970s Leverton's went out of the motor car business, and the garage was converted into a training centre, training people in the handling, and service of various pieces of mechanical handling equipment that the business had expanded into.

The main factory was in Westlode Street, where Caterpillar tractors were serviced and repaired. Also in Westlode Street was a tractor showroom for the display of new tractors. Another smaller factory was sited on the west side of Pinchbeck Road, and opposite this was a car showroom.

In March 1970 H. Leverton & Co. Ltd. became a member of the Unilever Organisation. By 1976 Leverton's was one of the world's largest and oldest Caterpillar dealers, operating from nine modern depots, strategically located throughout the country with an employment figure of around 1300. The new computer centre that they built in Westlode Street, opposite the main factory, assisted in the control of the many aspects of the business.

Leverton's also played an important supporting role in the extraction of oil and gas from the North Sea with a service base at Great Yarmouth. Caterpillar diesel and gas engines were maintained from this location as it had good transport facilities to the oil rigs.

In the 1990s the name of Leverton disappeared from Spalding when the business was taken over by Finning (UK) Ltd. The factory in Pinchbeck Road was vacated and sold some years ago, and the site is now occupied by a supermarket. Also long since gone is the car showroom in Pinchbeck Road, and this site is now occupied by the offices of Roythorn's Solicitors. In Broad Street the garage that later became Leverton's training centre is now occupied by the Spalding Further Education Centre.

The Peterborough Coal Company

The Peterborough Coal Company had offices at 6, Sheep Market in 1919 but by 1922 they had moved to 10, Market Place and were still there in 1926.

Peterborough Coal Company's horse and cart fully laden at their coal yard in St. John's Road. Across the top of the picture can be seen the footbridge over the railway from Green Lane to St. John's Road.

Samuel Ernest Robinson, Motor body builder and painter

Samuel Ernest Robinson of The Green, Westlode Street, was in business in the 1930s as a motor car body painter, and car body builder. He also did repairs and signwriting. Samuel Robinson's was recorded in Kelly's Directory of Lincolnshire for 1933 and 1937.

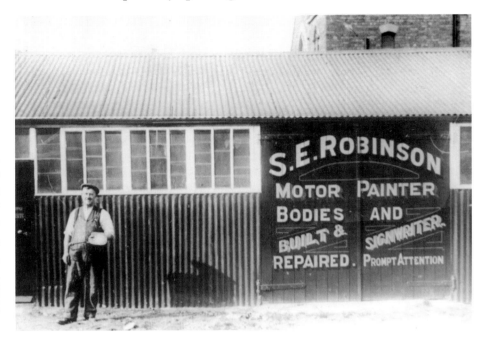

Charles Carter, horse slaughterer

Charles Carter of 22, Swan Street was in business as a horse slaughterer before 1908 and was still recorded in Kelly's Directory for the year 1919. He was not shown in the 1922 Directory, so it must be assumed that he had retired from that line of business by then.

H. Facer, harness maker

Harry Facer had his harness makers business at 6 London Road. In this photograph taken in June 1906 the proprietor can be seen stood in the shop doorway with his young assistant.

The property is now the printing works of Elsam Cross & Co. in London Road.

John Harrod, confectioner, 11 Vine Street

John Harrod of 11, Vine Street was listed in Kelly's Directory of 1900 as a clothier, but by 1905 he had become a confectioner and remained in that business until the mid-1930s making their own confection for retail and wholesale trade.

Advert dated 1933.

Harry Reeks, Veterinary Surgeon, Red Lion Street

Mr H. Caulton Reeks, F.R.C.V.S. of Spalding was one of the best known veterinary surgeons in the country. He started his practice in premises in Red Lion Street that is now the bakery shop of Paceys, but in 1918 he moved further up the street to a new purpose built building.

Harry Reeks died suddenly on 5th April 1937.

Harry Reeks, Veterinary Practice, in Red Lion Street, before 1918.

Harry Reeks about to go on his rounds. About 1915.

The buildings in Red Lion Street that Harry Reeks had built in 1918 for his veterinary practice. Photographed in 1988 before they were demolished.

Harry Reeks with his parents and family. About 1915.

Joseph Arnold, "Dr. Joe". Gentlemen's Hairdresser

Joseph Arnold, or "Dr. Joe" as he was known to the people of Spalding was a gentlemen's hairdresser who had his shop at 46 Albion Street.

By the year 1934 he had been a hairdresser for 62 years, and had accumulated 52 years membership of the Loyal Perseverance Lodge of Oddfellows (Manchester Unity). In this time he had only drawn three weeks sick pay Dr. Joe was well known as a fund raiser for the Johnson Hospital in the 1930s, before the days of the National Health Service, when local fund raising was very helpful to the financing of hospitals.

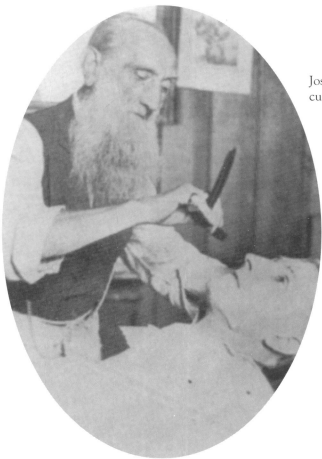

Joseph Arnold shaving a customer.

"Dr. Joe" on his decorated tricycle outside the Lincoln" Arms public house in Bridge Street, near the High Bridge. 1930s.

Branton & Co. china & earthenware factors

Messrs Branton & Co. had their pottery warehouse in Bedford Place in the 1930s. This warehouse is now the Granary Nightclub.

Molsons Chemists Ltd., 6 New Road.

For over half a century the Molson family served the people of Spalding with their chemists shop at 6 New Road.

In Kelly's Directory of Lincolnshire for the years 1900 and 1905 the business was recorded as being Talbot (The) Herbal Remedies Co. Ltd., Chemists.

By the time the 1919 Directory was published the business had been taken over by Algernon H. Molson, and he is recorded in the 1922 and 1926 Directories.

In the 1933 Directory the business was in the hands of A. H. & G. A. Molson, opticians and chemists.

After the war years the business was run for a long period by brothers George and Jack Molson.

Eventually the local authority expressed a desire to purchase the property to widen the entrance to Swan Street which was very narrow, and unable to handle the increased volume of traffic.

A new purpose built optician's premises was erected on land that had previously been occupied by Greenalls furniture business, that had been demolished. These premises were taken over on completion by Mr. Robert Molson who had entered the business some years earlier as an optician. The two brothers had retired, and the old shop was eventually demolished, and the road widened.

Molson's chemist shop in New Road.

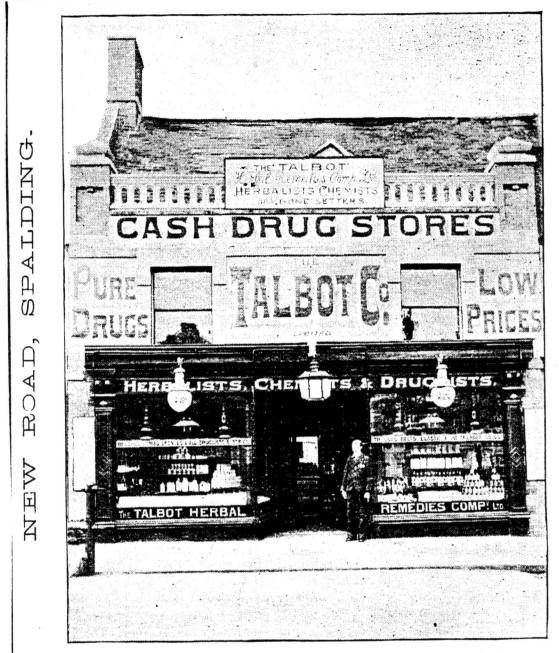

Talbot's chemist shop in New Road from an advert of 1902

The inside of Molson's chemists shop.

Swan Street after the road was widened. Where the chemists shop once stood is now roadway. The opticians premises is the new building on the right.

The Cattle Market.

Until 1938 the sale of livestock took place in various parts of the town. Sheep were sold in the Sheep Market from purpose built pens. Cattle were sold in New Road where holding pens were erected for Market Days. At the corner of Red Lion Street and New Road there were scales for the weighing of cattle. Pigs were sold in the yard at the rear of the Black Bull Inn that stood in New Road between Red Lion Street and Hall Place.

In 1937-38 a new purpose-built cattle market was erected off Swan Street. The complex was spacious, and the most up-to-date in the country. The pig pens were under cover, and there was two loading ramps for the loading and unloading of lorries. There was a large area of cattle pens with an undercover sales ring. In another part of the market were facilities for penning poultry ready for auctioning. The market also had offices for the use of the various auctioneers, and a canteen to provide sustenance for all who attended on market days.

The last market to be held on the streets was on 11th October 1938, and the new market was officially opened on Friday, 14th October, 1938.

Some years after the war additional buildings were erected within the market complex, and local auctioneers got together, and set up a bulb and produce auction.

With the passing of time support for the market dwindled, and on the 19th May, 1992, Spalding had its final Livestock Market after being on the Swan Street site for 54 years.

In May 1995 the bulb and produce auction moved to new purpose-built premises in Enterprise Way, and now trades under the title of Spalding Auctions.

The whole market was demolished, and the site was used to build the Holland Market shopping complex on.

View of Spalding Cattle Market taken from the Chatterton Water Tower.

The fully-enclosed cattle sales ring. This building has now been re-erected at Birch Grove Garden Centre and is used as a bulb museum.

Cattle pens.

Spalding Bulb and
Produce auction halls in
Swan Street.

The market canteen.

Unloading ramps where the pigs were taken off the lorries.

Pig pens. The boards running across the pens were for the auctioneers to stand on when selling.

Scales for weighing pigs and sheep.

Breweries
&
Public
Houses

There are no records as to where or when the first public house was founded, but before the invasion of Britain by the Romans ale was being brewed here. The ingredients of ale consisted of malt, which was made mainly from barley, yeast and water. It was not until sometime into the fifteenth century that the beverage was improved with the introduction of hops, and it was around this time that the drink became known as beer.

As to how early the population around Spalding had ale or beer available to them nobody really knows, but it can be almost certain that the drink was in use in this area as early as anywhere. The supply of wholesome water in this area was not available until about 1860. Before the introduction of tea and coffee the main drink for most people was beer.

Much beer before the nineteenth century was home brewed, and nearly all public houses brewed their own.

In July 1792, Thomas Hawkes made a list of the inhabitants of Spalding and their professions. This list records four brewers in the town:

1. Bennett, Richard – Brewer, Limeburner and Brickmaker.
2. Burwell, George – Brewer.
3. Boothe, George – Victuler and Common Brewer – White Lyon.
4. Glasspoole & Co. – Common Brewer.

Pigot & Co's Commercial Directory of 1830 also records four brewers:

1. Bugg Henry & Son, Cowbit Road.
2. Carter John R., Double Street.
3. Dean Henry, Crackpool Lane.
4. Robinson James, Cowbit Road.

It is thought that James Robinson's brewery in Cowbit Road was sited at the junction of Cowbit Road and Love Lane, because it is recorded that in 1856 Wensor and Eldred owned the Victoria Brewery that was in this position, but there was no record of Robinson being in business by then. Therefore it is a fair assumption that these people took over Robinson's brewery.

Not much is known about the brewery in Crackpool Lane, owned by Henry Dean, but it is known that in 1826 a brewery in Crackpool Lane was owned by Mills and Holeywell, and in 1842 a brewery was owned by John Penford Harvey, so it appears to have had several changes of ownership. John R. Carter of Double Street owned the Albion brewery, but it was only in existence for twenty years. It was built in 1824 and was quite large. Obviously the business did not give its owner the return he wanted, and he sold it to Bugg's on 6th April, 1846.

Albion Brewery from a Watercolour by Hilkiah Burgess 1827 (Spalding Gentlemen's Society Collection).

Breweries & Public Houses

The most successful brewery in Spalding was built by Henry Bugg in 1809, about 100 yards south of the Love Lane, Cowbit Road junction. Some years later Henry's son also named Henry joined the business, and it became very successful, which allowed them to live in Westbourne House, the grand abode that stood in front of the brewery, facing onto Cowbit Road.

Westbourne House with warehouse standing beside it. Photographed about 1948.

Westbourne House photographed in the late 1950s after the warehouse and chimney had been demolished.

Brewery Yard about 1948.

33

More Aspects of Spalding

Henry Bugg had other business interests besides the brewery. He had his own boat for the importing of wines and spirits, and he also set up the private bank of Bugg & Co. which had its head offices in Spalding. The bank closed in 1831 and a year later the partners became shareholders in the Stamford, Spalding and Boston Banking Co. Ltd. This bank was eventually taken over by Barclays Bank about the year 1900. Young Henry Bugg took over the brewery from his father in the early 1840s. Young Henry retired about 1872 and his son Joseph H. Bugg took charge of the brewery. Henry the Younger died in 1876, and at the end of that year, Joseph changed his name from Bugg to Burg. By the year 1892 Joseph had retired and sold the business to Soames & Co. Sometime after this Westbourne House became used as offices for the brewery, and remained in that use for many years. Soames & Co. was eventually taken over by Steward and Patteson, and some years after this Watney Mann became the owners, but brewing had ceased some years earlier.

List of property owned by Henry Bugg the younger from the schedule of his will thought to have been drafted in 1874:

Brewery, Cowbit Road, Spalding.
Together with Steam flour mill and engine. Four pair of French stones, Engine gear, Dressing machines, Ricing sieves, Small steam engine, pumps etc. Three iron tanks, Stout house, spirit and ale stores, Rooms, Stables, Sheds, Coach house and Office. Large malting and gardens. Own house and fixtures.

George and Dragon Inn, Peterborough.

Rose and Crown Inn, Peterborough.

Horse and Jockey Inn, Peterborough.

Red Lion Inn, Eye.
together with land.

Blue Boar Inn, Cowbit.
Together with Wheelwrights shop, Cottage and Land.

Plough Inn, Deeping St. Nicholas.
Together with six cottages, Blacksmiths and Wheelwrights shop and Land.

Man and Horse Inn, Moulton Eaugate.
Together with three cottages, Blacksmiths shop and Land.

Red Last Inn, Whaplode Drove.
Together with new cottages, Blacksmiths shop and Land.

Plough Public House, Windcatch, Low Fields.
Together with about 1 acre of Land.

George and Dragon Inn, Holbeach Road, Spalding.

Pigeon Inn, Holbeach Road, Spalding.
Together with Stables, Shoe Makers shop and Coal Yard.

Bell Inn, Moulton.
Together with Stables, Cottage and Land.

Breweries & Public Houses

Red Lion Public House, Pinchbeck.
Together with cottage and gardens

Punch Bowl Inn, New Road, Spalding.

Oat Sheaf Inn, Deeping St. Nicholas.
Together with Five cottages, Blacksmiths shop and Land.

Chequers, Winsover Road, Spalding.
Together with a cottage in the yard.

Crown Public House, Spalding.
Together with Cottage and Pigsties.

Gate Public House, Holbeach Road, Spalding.
Together with Garden Lands.

Masons Arms Public House, Moulton.
Together with Garden.

Crooked Billett Public House, Fleet.
Together with Stables and Blacksmiths shop.

Plough Public House, Moulton Chapel.
Together with Stables and Garden.

Black Bull Public House, Crowland.
Together with Stables.

Wheat Sheaf Public House, Dowsdale, Whaplode Drove.
Together with Land.

Bell Public House, Weston Hills.
Together with Bake House.

Peacock Public House, Pinchbeck.
Together with Stables.

Bell and Bowl Inn, Whaplode.
Together with Stables and Garden.

Ram Inn, Holbeach Drove.
Together with Shop and Garden Land.

Loggerheads Public House, Double Street, Spalding.

Bell Public House, Thurlby.
Together with Land.

Jolly Crispin Public House, Lutton.
Together with Shop, Stables and Land.

Red Cow Public House, Quadring.
Together with Cottages, Stable and Garden.

Land and two Cottages on Cowbit Road, Spalding.

Soames & Co.'s pop bottling plant at the brewery in Cowbit Road about 1950.

After changing ownership several times the brewery, which had become nothing more than a storage depot with offices, closed completely and the whole site was closed. Westbourne House was converted back to living accommodation, becoming two houses. Langton House adjoining was made into flats, and the cottages next door were modernised. After the brewery yard was cleared a new road was laid, Westbourne Gardens, and new houses were built on the site.

Three-storey Langton House and the brewery cottages. Photographed about 1948.

Another property on this site that was owned by the brewery was the Tower House. The origins of the house and tower are obscure, but it is thought to have been built in the early Victorian times. It is doubtful if the tower had ever served any useful purpose other than to be "somebody's folly", as had been the fashion in the Victorian era. It was said that on a clear day Boston stump could be seen from the top. The tower had to be demolished in 1963 as it became unsafe, and the house fell into a very dilapidated state. Had it not been for local builder Mr. Geof Sharman the house would have totally disappeared, but he saw the ruin as a challenge, and rebuilt the house just as it was when it was first built, but without the tower.

Tower House is now Mr. Sharman's own private residence.

Tower House complete with tower about 1958.

The Star Inn, Cowbit Road.

Next door to the brewery, at one time, stood a very unusual house called the Star Inn, thought to have been built about 1583 from the ruins of Spalding Priory. Until the middle of the seventeenth century this was said to have been the Poor House.

The building was a low thatched house, with porch, and a gabled room over it. In 1719 the owner at that time a Mr. William Atkinson, solicitor, gave the Inn to the Governors of Spalding Grammar School.

With the passing of time the Star Inn became very dilapidated internally and externally, and was nothing more or less than a beggar's opera.

By the late 1870s Joseph Burg, who by this time had changed his name from Bugg to Burg had a desire to extend his garden, and being aware that the Governors of the Grammar School wanted to build a new school, he came to an arrangement whereby he gave them some land in Priory Road in exchange for the old inn. The Inn was demolished in 1880 and Joseph Burg had the old arched entrance to the Inn re-built into his garden wall, nearly upon the site that it formerly stood.

The Star Inn, Cowbit Road from a watercolour painting by Hilkiah Burgess, 1848. Spalding Gentlemen's Society Collection.

The old arched entrance to what used to be the Star Inn. Re-erected in almost its original position.. Photographed 1998.

The Star Inn, Cowbit Road, shortly before it was demolished in 1880.

The Plough, Windcatch Corner, Low Fulney.

On the last Tuesday in September 1964, the last pint was served in the old Plough Inn at the Windcatch Corner, Low Fulney, and 200 years of history came to a close. The licensee, 71 years old Mrs. Jessie Goddard decided to call it a day after the death of her husband. Although the building was famous for having a resident ghost, it did not make an appearance, leaving the celebrations to the 15 or so regulars who spent the evening remembering the many good times that they had enjoyed. The plough appropriately named for an agricultural area, served as a local for the people who worked on the Land Settlement, and some of those attending on the last evening had been regulars for more than a quarter of a century.

The public house which also had with it a little over an acre of land was eventually demolished, and the land was incorporated into the adjacent field, so that today no trace is left of where the Plough once stood.

The Plough at the Windcatch from a watercolour painting by Hilkiah Burgess, 1820. Spalding Gentlemen's Society Collection.

The Plough at the Windcatch. Photographed in the summer of 1952.

The site where the Plough used to stand. Photographed 1994.

The Nags Head, Double Street.

Some of the public houses in Spalding in the 19th century, especially those close to the river left much to be desired. In the 1870s the Nags Head in Double Street was a popular lodging house, and was a very rough spot. It was in March 1882, that the then landlord was summonsed for keeping a disorderly house, and the licence was forfeited. The owner Mr M. W. Coward, brewer, of Boston, appealed against the decision and lost, and the house was closed. In the following September, Mr. Coward applied for a renewal of the licence, Canon Moore, Vicar of Spalding, who was on the Bench, reminded him that this was scarcely a reasonable request after he had involved the county in £20 expenditure, through compelling them to resist his appeal. Mr. Coward promptly retorted that, if the Bench would renew the licence he would recoup them the £20. Mr. Coward's clever challenge secured him the licence, and a cheque for £20 was placed in the Johnson Hospital box on the Sessions House table.

In February 1907 the story partly repeated itself when the Brewster Sessions at Spalding again recommended the closing of the Nags Head.

From Slater's Directory 1849
Nags Head – Edward Palmer, landlord, Double Street
From Whites Directory of Lincolnshire. 1872.
Nags Head – Edward Palmer, landlord, Double Street.
From Whites Directory of Lincolnshire. 1892.
Nags Head – James Greaves, landlord, 63 Double Street

The Black Bull Inn, New Road.

The Black Bull Inn situated on the south side of New Road went back many years, and in its early days would have overlooked the River Westlode, that flowed down the centre of where New Road is in an east-west direction. When the cattle market was held in New Road, prior to October 1938, this Inn would have been very busy serving the people attending the market.

On 22nd June, 1739, when the Black Bull Inn was kept by Mr. Matthew Everard, the Black Bull Lodge of the Freemason's was founded in this inn, where it held its meetings until it was officially erased from the Grand Lodge in 1754.

The Black Bull Inn became very run-down in the 1960s, and so some years later the Inn was closed down and demolished, and three new shops were built on the site.

The Black Bull Inn, New Road, photographed about 1950.

The Angel Inn, Double Street.

The Angel Inn in Double Street was a very old hostelry, well known for serving the mariners who once sailed in and out of the port of Spalding. The Inn was very old, being mentioned in the memorandums of Thomas Hawkes, recorded in July 1792, when the landlord was given as John Clark. Pigot's Directory of 1830 still lists John Clark as the occupant. Whites Directory of Lincolnshire for 1892 lists the landlord as John Turner. The Angel, 35, Double Street. Captain Turner was also a barge owner. By 1937 Kelly's Directory gives the landlord as Fred Oliver Levesley, and he too had connections with the sea. One of his ancestors Captain George Levesley was skipper of Mr. Henry Bugg's vessel in the 1830s,

The Angel Inn was left unoccupied for many years, and fell into a very bad state of repair. In the 1990s the old Inn was converted into three modernised dwellings under the riverside re-generation scheme.

The Angel Inn about the year 1900.

Three modernised dwellings that were once the Angel Inn. Photographed 1999.

43

The Pigeon Inn, Holbeach Road.

The Pigeon Inn in Holbeach Road served the community in that area for over 200 years, as well as the mariners who would have moored their vessels at the nearby warehouses. Being situated on the main road out of Spalding towards Holbeach, this Inn must have seen much trade in days gone by. The Inn ceased trading in the late 1990s, and has now become a Chinese Take-Away.

The Pigeon Inn, Holbeach Road. Photographed 1950.

Adjacent to the Inn can be seen the warehouses of G. F. Birch & Son Ltd. On the 9th June 1964 the local press gave the following report regarding the warehouses:–

Memory of River Traffic

The tallest of the two "Pigeon" granaries near the Pigeon Inn, Spalding is being demolished. The granaries and a warehouse were offered for sale recently by Messrs G. F. Birch and Son Ltd., but have not been bought. The tallest granary is being pulled down as it was considered unsafe. The premises were used in the days when barges came up the River Welland to Spalding, but it is not known how old they are. The granary under demolition has not been used for four years.

The Wok Inn, Chinese Take-Away that has taken over the Pigeon Inn. Photographed 1999.

The George and Dragon Inn, Holbeach Road

The George and Dragon was another Inn that at one time stood in Holbeach Road, and not more than a hundred yards from the Pigeon Inn.

This establishment must have been in business for at least 100 years either as an Inn or in earlier days as a beer house.

In February 1907 the licensing justices revoked the licence on the George and Dragon as the inn was then redundant.

The George and Dragon Inn with Lansdowne House standing next door. In the background can be seen the row of cottages that once stood at the entrance to Roman Bank.

Holbeach Road in the year 2000. Lansdowne House is in the centre of the picture, and the George and Dragon Inn would have been stood to the right of the house. Notice the cottages no longer stand in Roman Bank.

Cottages that stood next door to the George and Dragon Inn with their inhabitants. About 1900.

The Millstone Public House, St. Thomas's Road

The Millstone public house in St. Thomas's Road started its life as a beer house sometime in the third quarter of the nineteenth century. As the beer houses disappeared it became a public house serving the people close by as a 'local'. The public house closed sometime around 1970, and later became offices for "Live Promotions", serving as this until the building was demolished in the year 2000 to make room for the car park of supermarket "Aldi".

The Millstone Public House, St. Thomas's Road, Spalding. Photograph 1950. The wooden shed on the right was a shoe repairers (Mr. Willerton).

The Millstone public house building shown here as the offices of Live Promotions. Photographed 1993. This building was demolished in the year 2000 to make room for the Aldi supermarket car park.

The Ancient Briton, London Road.

The Ancient Briton started off as a "Beer House" in the second half of the 19th century. White's Directory of 1892 gives the name of Frederick William Goodwin as the landlord. In 1899 the tenancy was taken over by Henry Bennett who also started up his butchery business from the premises. Henry and his son Burton carried on the butchery business from the Ancient Briton until 1914 when they moved to premises in Winsover Road where the business is still run by the family of the founder.

In 1919 the landlord was Harry Fall who remained landlord for some years. By 1937 the Ancient Briton had become fully licensed as a public house and the landlord was Herbert Gibbons.

The Ancient Briton in London Road, about 1900 when H. Bennett & Son ran their butchery business from the premises.

The Ancient Briton in London Road, about 1950.

The Ancient Briton eventually closed down and together with some cottages each side was demolished. These modern flats were built on the site. The flats have been called Briton Court, thus retaining the name of the old public house.

The Bull Inn, Churchgate.

The Bull Inn, Churchgate.
Photographed 1955.

There has been a Bull Inn in Churchgate since the early 1800s and probably before. In White's Directory of 1826 the landlord was listed as John Leach, and it appears to have remained within the Leach family for some years as White's Directory for 1842 lists the landlord as a William Leach.

The Bull was quite a small Inn and for many years was affectionately known by locals as the "Little Bull'. In the early 1960s the brewery decided to build a new public house on ground to the side and behind the Little Bull. The new Bull which cost £40,000 to build was completed, and opened to the public in 1965, and the old Bull Inn was demolished, leaving the town with a new attractive public house.

White's Directory 1826. Bull – John Leach, near High Bridge.
Pigot & Co.'s Directory 1830. Bull – John Leach, High Bridge.
White's Directory 1842. Bull – William Leach, High Bridge.
Slater's Directory 1863. Bull Inn – John Harrison Allen, Cowbit Road.
Kelly's Directory 1905. Bull Inn – Frank Renshaw, Churchgate.
Kelly's Directory 1919 and 1922. Little Bull Inn – Thomas Martin Pearson, Churchgate.
Kelly's Directory 1937. Bull Inn – Frank S. Lynch, Churchgate.

The Bull Inn, Churchgate.
Photographed 2001.

The Chequers Inn, Swan Street

The Chequers Inn is situated at the junction of Swan Street, Winsover Road and Station Street. It is an old Inn and goes back at least 200 years and probably further.

Although this building has been restored over the years it has still kept its original basic outlines. When you compare the present day photograph with the watercolour that was made of the Inn in 1855 by Hilkiah Burgess the similarity can be seen.

White's Directory 1826. Chequers – Abraham Pridgeon, Bourne Street.
White's Directory 1842. Chequers – Robert Christian, Winsover Road.
Slater's Directory 1849. Chequers – John Cotton, Winsover Road.
Kelly's Directory 1861. Chequers. – John Cotton, Bourne Road.
Morris's Directory 1863. Chequers. – John Cotton, Bourne Road.
White's Directory 1892. Chequers Inn. – George Whiers, Winsover Road.

Note: In the 1800s Winsover Road was sometimes referred to as Bourne Road, and it appears that for many years the Chequers was considered to be in Winsover/Bourne Road. Eventually in the 1900s it was decided to number it 1 Swan Street and it is still that today.

The Chequers Inn from a watercolour painting by Hilkiah Burgess painted in 1855.
(Spalding Gentlemen's Society Collection).

The Chequers Inn, 1 Swan Street.
Photographed about 1950.

The Chequers. Photographed in 1988.

Welland Inn, London Road

Records show that the Welland Inn has been in business for more than 150 years. In the 1840s it was listed in the Directories as the Welland Cottage, and it is not until the early 1900s that the building was classified as an inn. Before this it is likely that the Welland was a beer house and not licensed to sell wines and spirits.

The Welland Inn, London Road in 1919.

White's Directory 1842. Welland Cottage – Samuel Carey, London Road.
Slater's Directory 1849. Welland Cottage – Samuel Carey, London Road.
Kelly's Directory 1905. Welland Inn – Frank Hubbard, London Road.
Kelly's Directory 1919 and 1922. Welland Inn – Arthur Warnes, London Road.
Kelly's Directory 1937. Welland Inn – William Musgrave, London Road.

The Barge, Commercial Road

The Barge Public House at 96 Commercial Road, as its name illustrates, was a public house from the days when the river was busy with boats. It is photographed here about 1950. The house closed down some years later and was eventually demolished. New houses now occupy the site where it stood but the name lives on as the small estate is called Barge Close.

The Railway Tavern, Winsover Road

In the 1800s many of the public houses around Spalding were only licensed to sell beer, but as the century passed more houses found the need to sell wines and spirits, because of the increasing demand from their customers. Landlords had to apply to the Brewster Sessions for the necessary licence permitting them to extend the range of drinks that they sold to include wines and spirits as well as beer.

Not everybody by any means approved of public houses or the drinking of alcohol, and when applications were submitted for licences there was a certain amount of opposition as well as support for the licence to be granted. Much of the opposition came from Non-conformists and the various temperance associations.

The following article from the Spalding Free Press of 12th September, 1899 gives an example of how the applications were placed before the Justices.

The Railway Tavern:

The Brewster Sessions for South Holland were held at the Sessions House, Spalding, on Tuesday last, when there were present on the Bench: Rev. J. Russell Jackson, M.A. (Chairman), Rev. J. T. Dove, M.A., Rev. G. S. Leigh-Bennett, Dr. H. T. Stiles, Mr W. J. E. Hobson, Mr T. Atkinson, Mr R. Rose, Mr R. Merry, Mr Fitzalan Howard, Mr W. J. Thompson, and Mr J. T. Atton. A good deal of interest was attached to the proceedings, owing to the application of Mr. W. Ground for a wine and spirit licence for the Railway Tavern, Winsover Road, Spalding, this was being the licence which was granted by the Bench last year, and subsequently refused by the Licensing Committee. A considerable number of ladies belonging to the Spalding Branch of the British Women's Temperance Association were present in court, they having taken steps to oppose the granting of the licence.

The Annual Report.

Superintendent Osbourn presented his annual report as to the licensed houses in the division, as under: Police Station, Spalding, 5th September, 1899.

To the Chairman and Justices of the Holland Elloe Petty Sessional Division.
Gentlemen, – I have the honour to inform you that in this Petty Sessional Division, there are 159 ale houses, 95 beer houses, 8 beer houses for consumption off the premises, and 9 houses for the sale of wines and spirits by retail, making a total of 271 houses for a population of 36,500 giving one licensed house to every 135 of the population. The houses have been well conducted; one ale house keeper has been summoned for permitting drunkenness; and another for selling drink to a drunken person. Both cases were dismissed. Two have been convicted for selling adulterated liquor, and four for drunkenness or disorderly conduct. Twenty-four ale houses, ten beer houses, and three wine and spirit retailers have changed hands during the year. I have received two notices applying for fresh licences – one in Spalding from a beerhouse keeper for a full licence; and one for a house at Gedney Drove End, the latter being for really transferring the existing licence from old premises to new ones erected close by. The number of persons proceeded against for drunkenness during the year was 162. Of these 127 were drunk and disorderly, ten drunk in charge of horses and carts, ten simply drunk, and 15 drunk on licensed premises. Forty were strangers to the district.

The Railway Tavern Licence.
Mr William Ground, owner and occupier of the Railway Tavern, on Winsover Road, Spalding, applied for a wine and spirit licence, so as to make the house a fully licensed one. – Mr. J. G. Calthrop appeared on behalf of the application, which was opposed by Mr. Rothera, of Nottingham, who stated that he appeared primarily for the British Women's Temperance Association and through them for the congregations of Non-

Winsover Road before the year 1900. The building on the right of the picture was the Railway Tavern. This was demolished in the second half of the twentieth century and several shops were built on the site.

The Pied Bull Inn, Winsover Road, Spalding. Photographed about 1950. The property still stands but is no longer a public house but is used as living accommodation.

conformist churches in the town, and he also had a retainer from a number of owners of property in the locality.–

Mr. Calthrop stated that the application was practically the same as last year, excepting that the additional houses had been built, and it was arranged that in order to save the time of the Court, the Chairman should read over the notes of the proceedings taken by him on the last occasion. Mr. Calthrop now stated that during the past twenty years 227 houses had been built in the locality which would be served by this licence, and he put in two influentially signed petitions on behalf of the application. The signatures included those of five clergymen of the Church of England, one Roman Catholic priest, seven Churchwardens and Sidesmen, seven County Councillors, 12 Urban District Councillors and Guardians, two Overseers, two members of the School Board, and thirty teetotallers, including Mr. Hopper, who was one of the oldest teetotallers in Spalding. The petition was also signed by the oldest tradesman in Spalding, and Mr. G. Jarvis formerly superintendent of police. The signatures also included those of 330 householders resident in the district which would be served by this house. The total numbers of householders was 438, leaving 108 who had not signed.

The Chairman: Local Option. – Mr. Calthrop: Yes Sir, with local option we should win. – The other petition, from those outside the locality in question, bore 106 signatures. The locality, Mr Calthrop said, represented a population of one-ninth of the whole town, and he urged that the needs of the people could not be properly served by the two fully-licensed houses at present existing.

William Ground was called, and stated that he had obtained most of the signatures. He said that some people had come spontaneously to sign, and he had only had about a dozen refusals. He described the accommodation which would be afforded by his house, and said he had daily applications for spirits. In cross-examination by Mr. Rothera, he admitted that there were several fully licensed houses between his place and the Corn Exchange, and he put the distance at about ten minutes walk – The solicitor stated that he had that morning walked it in six minutes, and to the fully licensed house the other way – to the Pied Bull – he had walked in seven minutes – In answer to Mr. Calthrop, Mr. Ground stated that some customers had left him because he could not supply them with spirits. Mr. Rothera, in opposing the application, put in petitions signed at the Non-conformist places of worship, against the licence. The signatures were 83 from the Free Methodist Chapel, 39 Baptists, and 37 Primitive Methodists – 139 in all. A Salvation Army petition against the licence contained 120 signatures, and there were also petitions from the Christian Endeavour Societies, from the Wesleyan Chapel, signed by the minister on behalf of the congregation, from the British Women's Temperance Association, and from owners and residents. Mr. Rothera argued that there was no need for the licence, and pointed out that in the division there was one licence for 135 of the population, including children, and in Spalding town one for every 231. He submitted that the circumstances were the same as last year when the licence was refused, and on public grounds there was no justification for the application. He quoted from the report of the Royal Commission, which recommended that the number of licences should be largely reduced. Mr. Calthrop replied, and the Bench retired to consider the application. The Chairman, upon their return stated that of the eleven magistrates, two were neutral, six were in favour of granting the application, and three were against. As far as the court was concerned the licence would be granted. The matter will have to come before the Licensing Committee for confirmation. The Railway Tavern was eventually granted the necessary licence. By the 1930s all the public houses became licensed to sell wines and spirits besides beer, and the old-fashioned beerhouse passed into history.

The Peacock Inn, Pinchbeck Road

The Peacock Inn in Pinchbeck Road was originally quite a small building, but in the 1950s the brewery took over the next door property that was occupied as offices by Armstrong and Thompson who were produce merchants. This enabled them to enlarge the premises.

The Peacock has been an Inn for over 200 years. It was first mentioned in the Memorandums of Thomas Hawkes, that was drawn up in 1792 when the landlord was listed as a Mr. J. Cussins.

The Peacock Inn, Pinchbeck Road in 1951. The Inn is the small building behind the street lamp. To the left is the offices of Armstrong and Thompson produce merchants.

The Loggerheads, 20 Double Street

The Loggerheads in Double Street started its days as a Beer House. White's Directory of 1892 lists 20 Double Street as a Beer House the landlord being a Peter York. In Kelly's Directory of 1922, 20 Double Street is still listed as a Beer House and the landlord then was a John William Stanger.

It was not until Kelly's Directory of 1937 that the Loggerheads appears listed as a public house, and the landlord was William Elstob. In the 1950s Joseph W. Patterson was the landlord.

The Loggerheads was eventually demolished to allow the expansion of Leverton's factory.

For many years a well known character of Spalding named Peter York kept the Loggerheads beerhouse and lodging house in Double Street. He was the best known Chimney Sweep in the Spalding District and employed several men.

The sign at that time over the Loggerheads bore the following quaint verse:

The Loggerheads Public House – Photographed about 1950.

Peter York does live here,
He sweeps your chimneys not to dear;
And if by chance they get on fire,
He puts them out at your desire.

The Mail Cart, Pinchbeck Road

The Mail Cart in Pinchbeck Road was built in 1843. Being situated by the side of the road to Pinchbeck it has been popular with both locals and travellers alike.

For many years the Mail Cart was the home of the Parkside Tennis Club until the ground was needed for extra car parking. The Mail Cart Bowls Club has been highly respected by people interested in this sport, and the Club is still very active today.

In the 1990s the Mail Cart changed its name to the Royal Mail Cart.

The Mail Cart photographed in the 1930s with the landlord Joseph Fovargue stood outside.

The Mail Cart photographed in 1952.

The Royal Oak, Cowbit Road

The Royal Oak in Cowbit Road goes back about 200 years. In the 1930s the old thatched public house was demolished, and a new one built. It carried on trading as the Royal Oak until the year 2000 when new owners changed it to the Fenway.

The Royal Oak about 1920.

The Royal Oak about 1950.

The Crown Inn, Westlode Street.

The Crown Inn at 36 Westlode Street is shown here about 1950. Some time after this the Inn was demolished and a new private hotel was built on the site. The building is now a home.

Townscape

Naming of streets in Spalding.

Years ago the naming of streets was very haphazard, but the Improvement Commissioners took the matter in hand after having received a communication from the Registrar General, asking them to co-operate with them in sorting out the problem.

The following is an extract from the Minute Book of the Corn Exchange, Fire Engine and Cemetery Committee:

17th February, 1871. At a meeting of the Special Committee appointed by the Spalding Improvement Commissioners for the purpose of Naming the Streets and Numbering the Houses in the Town.

Present:
Mr. A. Maples,
Dr. Morris,   Mr. C. Caulton.

Mr. A. Maples was appointed Chairman of the Meeting.

The Committee having read the communication from the Registrar General strongly urging the co-operation of the Commissioners with him in facilitating public and also private convenience by Naming the Streets and numbering the Houses proceeded to consider the names to be given to the Streets on the west side of the River Welland and recommend as follows:–

Market Place as heretofore.
That from Mr. Hall's clothing shop round by Mr. Vickers shop, Dallicoats the Cross Keys and Yearing's shop to be called Hall Place.
Red Lion Street be still called by that name.
From Hall Place to entrance to Pinchbeck Street to be called New Road.
Pinchbeck Street to commencement of macadamized road.
Westlode Street from entrance to Pinchbeck Street to its junction with the Albion and Double Streets.
Albion Street from old Albion Brewery to Gas House.
Beyond Gas House, Marsh Road.
Double Street from Albion Street to Bridge Street.
Crackpool Lane, Broad Street and Herring Lane as heretofore.
Bridge Street from the High Bridge to the Market Place and to Vine Street corner.
London Road from last mentioned point (end of Bridge Street) to old Toll Bar House.
Welland Place, London Road from Garfit's Bank to Mr. East's corner both inclusive.
Upper Welland Terrace, London Road the row of houses occupied by Dr. Stiles, Mr. Hobson and others.
Lower Welland Terrace, London Road from Dr. Stiles to Spring Street.
Road to Parkinson's Pit, Water Lane.
From March railway crossing to Bourne Road, St. Thomas's Road.
Green Lane from St. Thomas's Road towards the crossings of the several railways.
Late Bretts Walk to be Spring Gardens.
Vine Street from Bridge Street to Hole in the Wall Passage.
From entrance to Hole in the Wall Passage to Sheep Market, Crescent.
Maples' Passage, Abbey Passage.
Hole in the Wall as heretofore.
Wiles Path, Abbey Path.
Sheep Market as heretofore.
Gore Street from Sheep Market to Willesby School.
Winsover Road from Willesby School to Old Toll Bar.

Bourne Road from Old Toll Bar to extremity of Parish.

Hawthorn Bank as before.

Chapel Lane as before.

Deadman's Lane to be called Swan Street.

On the east side of the River Welland the Committee recommend as follows:

That from the High Bridge to Love Lane be named Church Gate, and from Love Lane to end of Parish Cowbit Road.

Love Lane as heretofore.

Church Street as at present.

From Church Street to Barrell's Lane as before Halmer Gate.

From Church Street to Matmore Gate the old name of Stonegate.

From last road to Gate in Cunningham's or Childers Road as before, Matmore Gate.

From High Bridge to Albert Bridge, High Street.

From Albert Bridge to Allam's Tunnel, Commercial Road, Thence to Fulney Bridge, Holbeach Road.

Willow Row Walk from junction with High Street to Albert Street near Exeter Drain.

Road to left of Suters House to Mercers Row, Brewers Place.

Mercer's Row as heretofore.

Square at entrance to Mercer's Row from Vine Street, Mercer's Place.

The Committee also recommend that the following places have names given to them and the Houses numbered although they are not repaired by or under the control of the Commissioners as Highways:

Lane out of High Street at end of Dr. Morris' House, Bath Lane. Lane from Winsover Road to Hawkes', Mill Lane.

Lane from Crescent to Grassams House, Foundry Lane.

Street from Bourne Road by the side of Entrance to Great Northern Railway Station, New Bond Street.

Lane next Storr's House, Short Street.

Lane from Sheep Market and Square at bottom belonging to Mr. Henry Caulton, Malting House Square.

Lane at end of Whites' Factory in Sheep market, Gore Lane.

The New Road set out by Mr. Hawkes from St. Thomas's Road opposite Spring Gardens, Henrietta Street.

The street intersecting Henrietta Street to be called Cross Street.

Houses from Mercer's Row or Brewer's Place to Mr. Hobson's Garden, Orchard Street.

The Committee recommend that such names as are approved be at once put up in the manner prescribed by the act and that the houses and Buildings in each Street be also at once numbered consecutively.

That where a House and place of Business are occupied the one by a partner and the other by the firm the Committee recommend that the two buildings have separate and distinct numbers.

The Committee further recommend that Tenders be immediately invited for executing the work.

> A. Maples, Chairman.
> Confirmed.
> Febr. 24, 1871.
> M. Shadford,
> Chairman,

The Market Place.

Being rectangular in shape, and surrounded by high buildings, Spalding Market Place is quite impressive with its varying styles of architecture.

The oldest of the buildings would be the White Hart Hotel, said to date from the reign of Richard II or even before. Throughout its history the hotel has been a meeting place for various organisations, and the Market Room was popular with farmers and businessmen who took refreshment within its walls when attending the market. In the later part of the 19th century the White Hart Hotel was a popular place for people to come and stay. Arriving by train, the White Hart horse drawn coach would meet the guests at the station providing them with the hotel's personal transport.

Spalding Market Place about 1914. The White Hart Hotel is on the left without a canopy over the main entrance. This was added in 1916. The Market Place was cobbled.

The White Hart closed down in 1987 after having been bought by a developer together with some of the adjoining property with the intention of redeveloping the site as a shopping centre. As of the beginning of the year 2001 the White Hart is still empty, but some of the neighbouring property has been demolished and rebuilt. The White Hart is still waiting to reclaim its former position as a leading establishment in the Market Place.

The White Hart Hotel coach on Spalding Market Place, 1899. The coach was used to transport customers to and from the railway.

Male Employees outside the White Hart Tap Room, Spalding, April 1899.

The White Hart Hotel about 1950.

Close by is the Red Lion Hotel, not as old as the White Hart, but even so it goes back several hundred years, and is still a thriving and popular establishment. This hotel has also been a meeting place, and still is for various organisations.

The side view from Red Lion Street of the Red Lion Hotel. From a watercolour painting by Hilkiah Burgess about 1830. (Spalding Gentlemen's Society Collection).

Townscape

At the end of the Market Place stands the modern South Holland Centre, a building that has courted much controversy about its design and cost. The building that many people talk about with affection is the old Corn Exchange that was built in 1855-56 at a cost of about £2,500 and stood on this site for over 100 years. It was designed by Bellamy and Hardy of Lincoln, and built by William Sharman and Son of Red Lion Street, Spalding.

The Corn Exchange decorated with artificial tulips at Tulip Time about 1950.

Minstrel Show on the stage of the Corn Exchange.

Tea party being held in the Corn Exchange about the year 1900.

Townscape

As the name suggests the Corn Exchange was used for much of its life by farmers and seedsmen for the buying, and selling of corn on market days. Stands were set up so that the samples of the seed could be laid out for buyers to examine. The Corn Exchange also had many other uses. Frequently auctions of furniture and other household effects were held, and on special occasions the large hall was used for tea parties. The local Operatic and Dramatic Society used the stage for their various productions, and local tradesmen held exhibitions of the products that they sold. For over 100 years the Corn Exchange served the people of Spalding in many ways.

In 1972 the Corn Exchange was demolished, and the South Holland Centre built on the site.

Ever since the South Holland Centre was built in the 1970s there has been much controversy as to the appearance and design of the building. In 1996 the local authority decided to do major alterations to the building, and also build a complete new front, thus altering the whole front elevation. Almost two years later in 1998 the newly constructed South Holland Centre opened to the public again.

After almost thirty years since the Corn Exchange was demolished, and older people still speak of the building with much affection, there is no doubt it will be many a long while before it is forgotten.

The South Holland Centre photographed in the 1970s soon after it was opened.

The South Holland Centre photographed in 1999.

Spalding Market Place photographed about 1960.

Spalding Market Place in the 1950s. The octagonal wooden building near the ornamental street light was the Market attendants hut. To the left of the hut can be seen the Market Place pump.

Lloyds Bank photographed about 1900 soon after it was built.

The Market Place about 1930.

Trades and professions in the Market Place in 1937

Baker, Albert & Co. Ltd., tobacconist. 9 & 10 Market Place.
Barclays Bank Ltd., Market Place.
Boots The Chemist, 7 Market Place.
Burton, Montague Ltd., tailors, 9 & 10 Market Place.
Calthrop & Leopold Harvey, solicitors, 11 Market Place.
Corn Exchange, Market Place.
Curry's Ltd, cycle agents, 14 Market Place.
Donington & Co., wholesale chemist & dealer in decorating materials, 7a Market Place.
Easiephit Footwear Ltd., boot dealers, 11 Market Place.
Field, John W., grocer, 18 Market Place.
Fletcher, Wm., outfitter, 6 Market Place.
Freeman Hardy & Willis Ltd., boot & shoe makers, 4 Market Place.
Hardy, Alice (Mrs.), tobacconist, 25 Market Place.
Hunter's The Teamen Ltd., grocers, 2 Market Place.
Lloyds Bank Ltd, Market Place.
Massey, George & Sons, seed merchants, 17 Market Place.
Midland Bank Ltd., 8 Market Place.
Morris, S. & H. Ltd., wallpaper merchants, 3 Market Place.
National Provincial Bank Ltd., 22 & 23 Market Place.
Red Lion Hotel, Market Place.
Rippon, Jas., hairdresser, 2 Market Place.
Scupham, Charles Wardle, pork pie maker, 26 Market Place.
Spalding Standard (Lincolnshire Standard Ltd.). 14 Market Place.
Stephenson Smart & Co., accountants, 3b Market Place.
Timpson, William Ltd., bootmaker, 1 Market Place.
Toynton, Samuel, newsagent, 24 Market Place.
White Hart Hotel, Market Place.
Williams, Frank, fruiter, 5 Market Place.

Sheep Market

In the days of the Priory, the triangle of land that we know as Sheep Market was then known as the Gore. The word gore meaning a triangle of land, and the name has still been retained with the lane beside the present Post Office being called Gore Lane. This piece of land had the Priory walls forming a boundary on the southern side, and on the north was the River Westlode. In the distant past this waterway was very important as it was used for people and goods to be transported between Spalding and Bourne. Tournaments and plays were held on the Gore when Knights and Nobles would prove their skills against each other in a joust. Combatants would have pitched their tents around the Gore. When the spirit of chivalry died out the tournaments degenerated into sumptuous pageants and plays, the last one being held in the reign of Henry the Eighth. The Great Gate of the Priory stood where the entrance to the Crescent now is opposite the Sessions House.

Besides being used for entertainment the Gore was also the place where people set up stalls to sell their wares. By the 19th century the Gore had become known as the Sheep Market, and became the area where a thriving trade in sheep was done.

Until 1876 the Lords of the Manor of Spalding owned the market rights, but on the 19th January 1876, the rights were conveyed for the sum of £4,000 to the Spalding Improvement Commissioners. Also in 1876 Samuel Kingston, an auctioneer in Spalding erected permanent pens for the sheep to replace the temporary ones that were erected every week. The pens remained until 1938 when they were removed after the sheep market moved to Swan Street where the new market had been built. Since 1938 the area where the sheep were has been used as a car park.

BINGHAM AND TOWNSEND,

WHITE HART

COMMERCIAL AND

FAMILY HOTEL

And General Posting House,

MARKET PLACE, SPALDING.

OMNIBUSES MEET EVERY TRAIN.

OFFICE FOR PARCELS BY PASSENGER TRAINS.

Wedding Carriages, Hearse and Mourning Coaches, Shilliberes, &c., &c.

WHOLESALE AND RETAIL

WINE, SPIRIT, & PORTER

MERCHANTS, AND

GENERAL BREWERS.

AGENTS FOR THE SALE OF

PALE AND BURTON ALES, AND LONDON AND DUBLIN STOUT.

Advert for the White Hart Hotel 1860s.

Townscape

The Sheep Market had space for 1,300 sheep. Spalding April Fair was the biggest day of the year for sheep, and they had to accommodate them wherever they could. All the streets in the vicinity of the Sheep Market were used. In 1899 approximately 26,000 sheep passed through the market, averaging about 500 per week, but this would not have been as many as in earlier years as by this time the sale of fat sheep had greatly declined.

Old Houses in the Gore (Sheep Market) built out of the Abbey Ruins. From a watercolour painting by Hilkiah Burgess (Spalding Gentlemen's Society collection).

The view in 1998 of where the old houses once stood in the Sheep Market.

79

Remains of the Great Gateway to Spalding Priory.
From a watercolour painting by Hilkiah Burgess,
1815 (Spalding Gentlemen's Society collection).

This photograph was taken before 1884. On the right of the picture can be seen the House of Correction (Prison) built in 1826 at a cost of nearly £15,000. In 1851-2 the building was enlarged. The prison closed down on 31st March, 1884, and was sold for £1,800. On the left is the Sessions House that was built in 1842-3 at a cost of more than £6,000. The building was officially opened on 30th June 1843. In the foreground are the pens to accommodate the sheep on market days.

Sheep Market with the Pied Calf behind the Sheep Pens on the right. About 1900.

In this photograph it can be seen that the House of Correction has gone, and a selection of buildings have replaced it. This picture was taken after 1909. The building on the right was originally built as a Drill Hall in 1890, but the building was overcome with financial problems, and in 1909 H. Leverton & Co. Ltd. purchased it and converted it into a Motor garage. In the centre of the photograph it can be seen that houses have been built on the spare land between the Sessions House and the garage. The street that this created was given the name of Victoria Street, no doubt being named after Queen Victoria.

Sheep Market about 1900.

Sheep Market about the year 1912 with the newly built Post Office in the left of the photograph.

Townscape

The Regent Cinema was built on the site of Leverton's garage by the Spalding Picture House Co. Ltd., and opened to the public on 20th June, 1927. This cinema had seating for 850 people, and in the circle there was a number of double seats much appreciated by courting couples.

The Regent closed down on 2nd February 1959 and the Trustee Savings Bank was built on the site.

Regent Cinema.

View of Sheep Market taken from the balcony of the Regent Cinema about 1950. At the bottom left hand corner can be seen the Civic Restaurant that was built on the site where poultry was once auctioned. This restaurant was demolished and a shop built on the site.

83

Sheep Market showing the Sessions House, Sheep Pens, and the Regent Cinema, about 1930.

Pied Calf Public House in Sheep Market decorated for the Coronation of George VI, 1937.

The last pig being auctioned in Sheep Market on Tuesday the 11th October 1938
before the market moved to Swan Street.

Parade passing through Sheep Market on the occasion of Queen Victoria's Diamond Jubilee, 1897.

The offices of R. Longstaff & Co., in Sheep Market, 1926.

Sheep Market about 1910.

Trades and Professions in Sheep Market in 1937.

Allen, Harold W., registrar of births, deaths & vaccination officer, 2 Sheep Market.
Bean, Alfred & Son, house furnishers, 18 Sheep Market.
Binder, F. J. postmaster, Sheep Market.
Britannia's Portraits, photographers, Sheep Market.
Cash & Co. (W. & E. Turner Ltd.), boot & shoe makers, 14 Sheep Market.
Dodd, Frederick, police inspector, Sessions House, Sheep Market.
Dryden & Son, Jewellers, 13 Sheep Market.
Gyde, Alfred S., photographer, 5 Sheep Market.
Jones, Percy, boot & shoe dealer, 4 Sheep Market.
Longstaff, R. & Co., auctioneers & valuers, Sheep Market.
O'Brien, Edward Ltd., cycle agents, 16 Sheep Market.
Pied Calf, public house (Harold Stephenson), Sheep Market.
Prescott, R. J., confectioner, 6 Sheep Market.
Prudential Assurance Co. Ltd., 17 Sheep Market (upstairs).
Seymour, A. L. & Son, tobacconist, 17 Sheep Market.
Shearer, Horace, butcher, 15 Sheep Market.
Regent Cinema (Spalding Picture House Ltd.) Sheep Market.
White, J. T. & Son., fancy goods dealer, 8, 9, 10 & 11 Sheep Market.
White, Tom A., & Son, auctioneer & valuers, Sheep Market.

New Road

New Road was officially given its name on the 17th February 1871 at a meeting of the special committee appointed by the Spalding Improvement Commissioners for the purpose of naming the streets and numbering the houses in the town, although for many years before this the road had unofficially been called by that name.

Up to the early years of the 19th century the River Westlode flowed along the course that is now taken by Westlode Street and New Road. This river is thought to have gone back to Roman times. The main bridge over the Westlode was a wagon bridge situated in the middle of what is now New Road, almost opposite the end of Red Lion Street. This was used by the main road traffic between Spalding and Boston.

After the new steam pumps were erected at Pode Hole in 1824 the quantity of water flowing along the Westlode was very small, and consequently the water became stagnant and smelly, and it was found that the river's days of usefulness had gone. The bridges that spanned the river between the White Swan (today known as the Bass House) and the River Welland were demolished, and the river which was by then little more than a stream, was arched over in sections at various times.

Silt was brought from the Welland at a cost of a shilling per load, and the remaining part of the Westlode was filled in by the owners of adjoining property. Before this was done there was a road each side of the river. The north side was called Westlode side, and the south was Rosemary Lane. When the filling in was completed it made the road very wide, being made up of the width of the river, and the added width of the road each side.

At the same time that New Road was named the section from the junction of Albion and Double Street, and Pinchbeck Road was given the name of Westlode Street.

With New Road being very wide, the cattle market that was previously held at the Junction of Hall Place and Sheep Market was re-located, spreading along the length of New Road and into Westlode Street. Iron posts were positioned along both sides of the road so that the cattle could be tethered, and on market days the road was bustling with people and animals. The market continued to be held in New Road until 1938 when on Tuesday the 11th October the last cattle market was held before the market moved to a new purpose built complex in Swan Street.

Since the creation of the 'New Road' in the early 1800s the thoroughfare has been lined with a good selection of business establishments, including in the past, four inns, two motor garages, three fish and chip shops, and a variety of shops covering most of the popular lines of business. Today the garages have gone, but New Road still offers quite a selection of businesses. Only one fish and chip shop remains, but several other forms of fast food take-aways have opened up, and there are still three public houses trading.

Notes from the Press about the Beast Market.

February 1880.

The Beast Market: – In 1874, owing to frequent complaints from the public, the beasts were removed by order of the Improvement Commissioners from the Hall Place corner of the New Road to the other side of Swan Street, on the same road, about 25 yards lower down. After a protracted and lively discussion, in which a good deal of temper and personality was shown, the Commissioners decided at their last meeting, by the casting vote of the chairman, to have the beast brought back again to the corner. Since the removal of the beast in 1874 the vacant space has been let by the market inspector for various purposes, and has recently been extensively used for auction sales of wood. On several occasions the road has been so blocked up with wood as to be a great inconvenience and nuisance to the farmers, cattle jobbers, &c. Had a sufficiently broad roadway been kept clear down the centre no reasonable complaint could have been made.

Cattle in New Road for the
market. Before 1900.

Sunday School Parade passing along New Road, early 1900s.

Market Day scenes in New Road, June 1928.

View in New Road on the last day of the market before it moved to Swan Street, 11th October, 1938.

The last beast being auctioned in New Road at the end of Red Lion Street, 11th October, 1938.

More Aspects of Spalding

September 1894.

Spalding Cattle Fair. – Spalding September cattle fair, which is the most important of the year took place on Tuesday, when there was an exceptionally large show of both beasts and sheep. The best bullocks fetched up to £20 a head; strong stores, £15 to £18; beast a year and a half old, £10 to £12; in-calvers up to £21; and calving heifers, £15 to £18 a head. The best sheep made 60 shillings each; stores, 24 shillings to 38 shillings. No demand for horses except those of better class. Inferior animals were a drug in the market.

New Road near its junction with Pinchbeck Road about 1905.

New Road about 1938.

Great fire affecting businesses in the vicinity of New Road.

Shortly after 10 p.m. on Wednesday, July 11th, 1900, a great glow lit the sky over Spalding, and many thought a bonfire had been lit to celebrate the show that was then on. Soon, however, it was realised that a great fire was raging. For miles over the flat countryside the glare could be seen, and hundreds came to view the spectacle. The fire originated in a large wooden furniture warehouse belonging to Mr. Cole which was situated at the back of New Road which was at the rear of where the cattle market was held. With goods of such an inflammable nature the fire quickly assumed gigantic proportions, and the surrounding cottages were soon in great danger. The people frantically threw their belongings out into the street, and into the field behind, there was plenty of willing workers, until the whole looked like some weird fair.

The Spalding fire appliances were very antiquated, and with the short supply of water were unable to cope with the fire. The hydrant's puny stream went simply nowhere, and it was seen that the burning mass would go its own way. This it did, and the blaze spread rapidly. Mr. Beales cycle works was quickly burnt down and the machinery ruined. There was an invalid lying in a cottage in Swan Street, which was burnt out, but she was removed to safety, though with considerable difficulty. The bicycles from Mr. Beales shop were also removed, and much of the bedding and furniture from the house was saved, but badly damaged by fire and water. Mr. Greenall's shop was soon added to the raging flames, but plenty of willing hands helped to clear much of the stock away, and it was stowed in the street. Luckily the wind carried the flames away, and the front part of the premises was saved. Owing to the scarcity of water from the waterworks supply and the antiquated fire appliances little could be done, so the Bourne fire engine was telegraphed for. Everybody expected that the whole block would go, but the fire died away at about 1.30 a.m.

The scene of the fire was a memorable one that people did not forget, and the area of conflagration was large.

The loss was a heavy one with only partial coverage for insurance. Mr. Beales was uninsured, and so were the cottages. Mr. Greenall's loss was over £2,000, and Mr. Coles was very heavy.

The origins of the fire were a mystery. It was thought by some that fireworks were responsible, but others did not agree.

New Road in the 1930s.

The shop of Harry Taylor, watchmaker about 1930.

The Punchbowl Public House and Turner's Fish Café about 1950.

Parade in New Road on
the occasion of the
Coronation of George V,
22nd June 1911.

Parade formed up
outside Stanger's garage
in New Road, before
1914.

New Road about 1950 with
Chester's grocery shop
standing on the corner of
Broad Street.

Trades and Professions in New Road in 1937

Black Bull Public House (H. Joseph Lynn), New Road.
Bolton's Garage, motor engineers, 19 New Road.
Butters, John Ltd., pawnbrokers, 31 New Road.
Cawthorn Ivor R., fried fish dealer, 35 New Road.
Cherrington, Edward, cycle agent, 16 New Road.
Chester, Hayden, grocer 32 New Road.
Floyd, Thos. Harold, confectioner, 25 New Road and Stationers, 1 Pinchbeck Street.
Goulson, Frans. P., hairdresser, 4 New Road.
Greenalls, house furnishers, 9 & 10 New Road.
Guy, Jn. Thos., confectioner, 33 New Road.
Hansons, drapers, 24 New Road.
Jackson, M. B. & Co., dyers and cleaners, 25 New Road.
Knipe Fras. E., fried fish shop, 15 New Road.
Maples & Son, solicitors, 23 New Road.
Molsons (A. H. & G. A. Molson), chemists & opticians, 6 New Road.
Morgan, Lilian (Mrs.), confectioner, 3 New Road.
Neaverson, Leslie Ltd., radio dealers, 8 New Road.
Peacock Chas., cycle dealer, 26 New Road.
Punchbowl Public House (Geo. W. Hames), New Road.
Reeds Garage Ltd., motor car agents, New Road.
Sentance, Agnes May (Mrs.), draper, 28 New Road.
Short, Chas. Edward, registrar of marriages, 23 New Road.
Stanger, Walter Herbert, wireless dealer, 20 New Road.
Tarry, Jn. Wm., dairy, 34 New Road.
Taylor, Harry, Watchmaker, 21 New Road.
Toyne, Jn. Wm., butcher, 18 New Road.
Turner, David, baker, 17 New Road.
Watson, Hildreth (Miss), ladies outfitter, 1 New Road.
White Swan Public House (Mordecai Kempston), New Road.
Whyles, Florence (Mrs.), greengrocer, 14 New Road.
Wooldridge, Vera (Miss), confectioner, 13 New Road.

Night time scene in New Road in the 1950s.

Hall Place

To the north west end of the Market Place is a triangular area called Hall Place, so named because for over 230 years this is where the Town Hall stood. In the days when the Town Hall was first built, about 1620, this area of ground was referred to as the Hemp Market. The building was the gift of Mr. John Hobson of Spalding, and was a grand structure, the entrance to which was approached by a flight of steps. Underneath the hall were a number of shops that were let for rents, which were to be divided between the minister of the parish church, and the poor of the parish, one-fifth going to the minister, and four-fifths to the poor.

By 1853 the Town Hall and adjoining buildings were found to be in a dilapidated state, and so the Spalding Improvements Commissioners decided to demolish the building, leaving Hall Place a large open area rather like a small market place.

In 1855/56 a replacement for the Town Hall was built in the Market Place, and given the name of the Corn Exchange.

After the site of the old Town Hall was cleared the whole area was laid with cobbles. By the end of the 19th century the cobbled area in Hall Place became much used on market days when stalls were set up, and local auctioneers held auctions of farm implements, and other objects that people wished to sell. In those days it was common to hear people say that there was

The Town Hall in Hall Place from a Watercolour painting by Hilkiah Burgess (Spalding Gentlemen's Society Collection).

an auction on "the stones" as this was what people often referred to Hall Place as. This term disappeared after the cobbles were removed, and a traffic roundabout installed to ease the flow of vehicles passing through Hall Place. In more recent years the round-about has been removed, and today much of Hall Place is a traffic-free area between 10 a.m. and 4 p.m. with only the roadway on the north west side being open to vehicles.

Until the second world war much of the property in Hall Place dated back to the late 18th and early 19th century, but in May 1941 an air raid destroyed or seriously damaged much of the property on the western side.

Hall Place about 1920 showing the cobbled streets and the implements on the "stones".

The largest shop destroyed was that of Pennington & Son who had a large drapery business at 10 to 13 Hall Place. This occupied the site where Boots the Chemists and Barclays Bank now stand. Also destroyed were the shops of International Tea Co. Ltd. at number 6, Home & Colonial Ltd. grocers at number 7, Freeman Hardy & Willis, shoes and boot dealers at number 8 and J. C. Harris & Sons, watchmakers at number 9. Altogether this left a large amount of destruction for a small town like Spalding, but the determination of the business people showed through and within a short time temporary accommodation was found, and business did its best to carry on against the odds.

After the war the site where the shops were destroyed was re-built bit by bit as building materials that were in short supply became available. On the opposite side of Hall Place the Cross Keys Hotel was demolished, and a super market was built on the site. The druggist store of Super Drug now occupies this shop. To the north of Hall Place the shoe shop run by the Matthews family for many years closed down and the building was demolished in October 1985. A new shop was built on the site, and at first was occupied by the Electricity Company. This property is now occupied by the firm of Super Saver. Altogether much of Hall Place has been re-built, and those of the older buildings that are left have been much restored.

Hall Place photographed in June 1926. In the picture can be seen the shop of Pennington & Sons that was later to be destroyed by enemy action in 1941. Also destroyed was the tall building to the left of Pennington's occupied by J. C. Harris the watchmaker and also the next three properties.

Parade passing through Hall Place, August 1902, on the event of the celebrations of the Coronation of Edward VII.

Parade in Hall Place on the occasion of the funeral of Edward VII, 20th May 1910.

Hall Place about 1900.

Hall Place Chambers, the offices of S. &. G. Kingston, auctioneers, soon after it was erected in 1908.

Willcox the Butchers shop in Hall Place about the year 1900. Cattle are being driven by, and there is meat etc. on open display on the stall. Today this would be a public health officer's nightmare. This is now the butchery business of T. Law & Sons Ltd.

View of some of the shops in Hall Place. About 1950.

Trades and Professions in Hall Place in 1937

Atton & Son, Paint Merchants, 19 Hall Place.

Barrell & Son, Wine & Spirit Merchants, 35 Hall Place.

Blindells (1934) Ltd. Boot Dealers, 27 Hall Place.

Boston & District Savings Bank, Hall Place Chambers.

Colburn Harriet Jessie (Mrs.) Hairdresser, 31 Hall Place.

Cross Keys Hotel (Rt. R. Scott), Hall Place.

Fleming Reid & Co. Ltd., Hosier, 1 Hall Place.

Foster Brothers Clothing Co. Ltd., Clothiers, 2 Hall Place.

Freeman, Hardy & Willis, Boot & Shoe Makers, 8 Hall Place.

Gibbs George William & Sons, Boot & Shoe Makers, 22 Hall Place.

Hallam & Blackbourn, Grocers, 18 Hall Place.

Harris, J. C. & Sons, Watchmakers, 9 Hall Place.

Hepworth, J. & Son Ltd., tailors, 3 Hall Place.

Hodgson & Harris Co., Chartered Accountants, 22a Hall Place.

Home & Colonial Stores Ltd., Grocers, 7 Hall Place.

International Tea Co.'s Stores Ltd., Grocers & Tea Dealers, 6 Hall Place.

Kingston, S. & G., Auctioneers and Surveyors, Hall Place Chambers.

Law, Thos. & Son, Butchers, 25 Hall Place.

Lincolnshire, Boston & Spalding Free Press, Hall Place.

London Central Meat Co. Ltd., Butchers, 4 Hall Place.

London & Provincial Wine Co. Ltd., Wine & Spirit Merchants, 23a Hall Place.

Long, F., House Furnishers, 30 Hall Place.

Mann & Son, Clothiers, 34 Hall Place.

Matthews, Geo. & Sons, Boot Dealers, 20 Hall Place.

Nicholls (Fras.) & Baragwanath (Spalding) Ltd., Produce Merchants, 32 Hall Place.

Nixon, Geo. Jas., Outfitters, 15 Hall Place.

Perks Dairies Ltd., Grocers & Tea Dealers, 17 Hall Place.

Pennington & Son Ltd., Drapers, House Furnishers, Milliners & Ladies Hairdressers; Tea Lounge, 10-13 & 13a Hall Place.

Russell, Alan (R. A. Potter), Gowns, 32 Hall Place.

Savings Bank (Arnold H. Smith, Actuary), Hall Place Chambers.

Sketchley Dye Works, 26 Hall Place.

Smith, Thompson & Co., Chartered Accountants, Hall Place Chambers.

South Lincs. Wholesale Potato Merchants Association, Hall Place Chambers.

Stanwell, J. R. & Son, Tobacconist, 16 Hall Place.

Tomlin, William Montague, Clothier, 23 Hall Place.

Webster, E. L. & Co. Ltd., Boot Dealers, 21 Hall Place.

The Matthews family shoe shop shortly before it closed down.

Broad Street

At the corner of the Market Place close to the South Holland Centre is Broad Street, which leads through to New Road. From the Market Place the first building on the right hand side is the drapery store of Hills. This site was previously occupied by the Greyhound Hotel. When the hotel was demolished, the new store was built keeping the front of a similar style to the hotel.

Next to Hills is Elderkin & Son, Gunsmiths. This business is known nationwide amongst the shooting fraternity. When Elderkin's first started trading in this shop they were china and glass dealers. In those days a sign in the shape of a large teapot used to hang over the street,

Elderkin's shop about 1930.

Broad Street about 1900. Behind the iron railings and fancy gate posts on the right was Harrington House. The building next to this that comes right to the footpath was the house that later became the Norwood Hotel.

The car park at the corner of Herring Lane was where Harrington House once stood. Before this was demolished it housed the Council Rating Department. Next to this and also demolished was the Norwood Hotel which in earlier days before conversion had been a house.

Next to the Norwood was Dembleby House the home for many years of the Longstaff family, but now the offices of Knipe Miller solicitors.

Opposite to where the Norwood was is the club house of the Spalding Club. This gentlemen's club was erected on a site that had for more than 120 years been occupied by the theatre or better known as the Assembly Rooms. The Club House was opened to members on 9th August, 1875, having been built by Mr. John Moore, junior, of Spalding at a cost of £1,640 10s. 3d.

Further along the street, and you come to the grand building that is the home of the Spalding Constitutional Club. This building was formerly the Manor House, built in 1727 by Everard Buckworth (1693-1751), and remained in the ownership of the Buckworth family for many years. In 1911 a committee of the Conservative and Unionist party acquired the Manor House to serve as headquarters for the party throughout the division. Early in March of that year Alderman J. H. Bunting, a well-known agriculturalist, and an enthusiastic Conservative party worker, stated that he would present the Manor House to the Conservatives of the Spalding Division.

The Constitutional Club photographed in 1972.

View looking along Broad Street from New Road. Dembleby House can be seen in the centre of the picture. Photograph about 1930.

Further along Broad Street there are two buildings that one cannot fail to notice.

The first is the Wesleyan Methodist Church which was erected in 1886-87. It was in 1826 that the first Methodist Chapel was built in Broad Street, on the site that was once occupied by the House of Correction. This had been demolished a short time before to enable the first chapel to be built. In 1886 it was decided to build a new church. The church that we see today was built adjacent to the old chapel. This present church was opened for Worship on 3rd March, 1887. It was intended to use the old chapel as a schoolroom, but when the new church was completed it was decided to pull the old chapel down and build a new schoolroom in keeping with the new building.

The Wesleyan Methodist Church in Broad Street about 1900.

The other building that catches the eye is the museum and lecture room of the Spalding Gentlemen's Society that stands opposite the church schoolroom.

It was in 1710 that the Gentlemen's Society was founded by Maurice Johnson, making it one of the oldest learned societies in the country. The museum is, with the exception of the Ashmolean at Oxford the oldest in the country

In 1910 the present museum and lecture room in Broad Street was built to celebrate the bi-centenary of the founding of the Society, giving the members the first permanent meeting place.

The museum of the Spalding
Gentlemen's Society.
Photographed 1972.

It was in 1907 the Spalding Urban District Council were able to widen Broad Street at the end near the Market Place. The National Provincial Bank had just built a new bank in the Market Place, and the council were able to purchase a strip of land from the Bank, enabling them to widen the street. It was then, in 1907, that the Council changed the name from Crackpool Lane to Broad Street.

Cottages that once stood opposite the Manor House. Photograph before 1900.

Trades and Professions in Broad Street in 1937.

Constitutional Club Ltd. (Jn. Hy. Tateson, sec.), Broad Street.
East Midland Finance Co. Ltd., Elsom House, Broad Street.
Elderkin & Son, china & glass warehouse, 17 Broad Street.
Elsom, George, seed and bulb grower, agricultural agent and rope and cover manufacturer, Elsom House, Broad Street.
Greyhound Hotel (Bert Preston), Broad Street.
Hassock Winifred (Miss) A. T. C. L., teacher of music, attends Norwood Hotel, Broad Street.
Hockney, F. A. & L. (Misses), bakers, 19 Broad Street.
Leivu Leon, gown specialist, Elsom House, Broad Street.
Leverton, H. & Co., motor engineers, Broad Street.
Mayfield, Frank, tobacconist, 8 Broad Street.
Merry, Major, solicitor, 6 Broad Street.
Palmer, W. & J. E., fancy goods dealer, 15 Broad Street.
Peniston, Harry Holmes, music seller, 16 Broad Street.
Roythorn, Edmund W., solicitor, 5 Broad Street.
Spalding Club Ltd. (Thos. O. Mawby, chairman; E. W. Roythorn, sec.), Broad Street.
Spalding Gentlemen's Society (Ashley K. Maples, president), The Societies Museum, Broad Street.
Stevenson, Archibold G. Temperance Hotel, Norwood Hotel, Broad Street.
Trower, Thos. L.R.I.B.A., chartered architect, Elsom House, Broad Street.

Private Residents:

Longstaff, Joseph Henry, Dembleby House, Broad Street.
Seymour Alexander V., 9 Broad Street.

Bridge Street

Bridge Street stretches from the Market Place to its junction with Vine Street, and has seen some considerable changes in the last hundred years. The biggest one was the demolition of the large store belonging to Berrills Ltd. that stood on the side of the river at the end of Double Street. This business closed down in 1970, and the building when demolished allowed the widening of Double Street, and the eventual planting of the shrubbery on the river side. In the days when traffic flowed through the street it was well known for hold-ups, and the narrow footpath led to accidents occurring with pedestrians. It has been closed to traffic now for some years.

In the past there was a large variety of shops, and at one time there were four grocery establishments. As of the present time, the shop that has remained in the same line of business the longest is the Pharmacy shop of Lloyds which is opposite the High Bridge. Lloyds has been a Chemists and Pharmacists for over a hundred years, trading under several different names. Following this the next oldest business is Woolworths who have been in the present position for over sixty years.

Trades and Professions in Bridge Street in 1937

Ashwells (Harry Luck), printer, stationer & newsagents, 16 Bridge Street.

Black, Tom, butcher, 22 Bridge Street.

Brown, Alexander, hairdresser, 24 Bridge Street.

Claypole, Albert Luke, pianoforte dealer, 21a Bridge Street.

Dixon, Thos. Smith, grocer, 1 Bridge Street.

Garwell, H. & O., fancy drapers, 2 Bridge Street.

Hayes, H., fishmonger, 9 Bridge Street.

Lennards Limited, bootmakers, 21 Bridge Street.

Lincoln Arms Public House (Chas. R. Andrew), 4 Bridge Street.

Marriott, Frank, tobacconist, 20 Bridge Street.

Maypole Dairy Co. Ltd., grocers, 18 Bridge Street.

Melias Ltd., grocers, 25 Bridge Street.

Osbourn, E. Arden, chemists & druggist, 7 Bridge Street.

Pilkington, Wm. F., pork butcher, 3 Bridge Street.

Bridge Street in the 1920s.

Reno Valet Sevice Ltd., clothes cleaners, 20 Bridge Street.

Reynolds, Jn., tobacconist, 17 Bridge Street.

Star Tea Co. Ltd., 13 Bridge Street.

Watson, Geo. & Co. (Geo. Watson) boot repairs, 20a Bridge Street.

Woodcock, Arth. B., baker, 10 Bridge Street.

Woolworth, F. W. & Co. Ltd., bazaar, 15 Bridge Street.

Wright, Kate (Miss), ladies hairdresser, 5 Bridge Street.

Bridge Street in the 1930s.

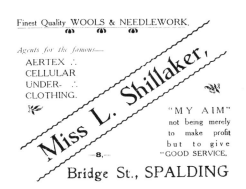

Finest Quality WOOLS & NEEDLEWORK.

Agents for the famous—
AERTEX ∴
CELLULAR
UNDER- ∴
CLOTHING.

Miss L. Shillaker,

"MY AIM"
not being merely
to make profit
but to give
"GOOD SERVICE.

Bridge St., SPALDING

View of some of the shops in Bridge Street from the opposite side of High Bridge. The shop with the ironwork across the top was Whiteman & Bell, chemists. The big building on the right of the picture was the shop of Berrills that was demolished in the 1970s.

Spring Gardens.

Connecting the Crescent with St. Thomas's Road is Spring Gardens. This road was formerly known as Brett's Walk as Mr. Brett lived in the only house that the walk then possessed. The name was changed to Spring Gardens at a meeting of the Special Committee appointed by the Spalding Improvement Commissioners for the purpose of naming the streets, and numbering the houses in the town on the 17th February 1871. Although not officially in Spring Gardens, the Post Office sorting office was previously the site of the United Methodist Free Church, which fronted onto the Crescent, with the side of the building taking up quite a footage along Spring Street. This fine majestic building was built on the site of a previous smaller chapel in 1878-79. The opening service at the new church was conducted by the Rev. John Adcock, of Manchester, on 22nd May 1879. Throughout the life of the Crescent church many influential Spalding people were members of the congregation.

Because of serious structural defects in the building, and the re-organisation of Methodism in Spalding it was decided that the Crescent Church should close. The final service was held on 22nd May 1955. The building was sold, and then demolished to make way for the building of the Post Office sorting office.

The United Free Methodist Church in the Crescent. About 1900.

Inside the Crescent
Methodist Church, decorated
for Harvest Festival,
September 1953.

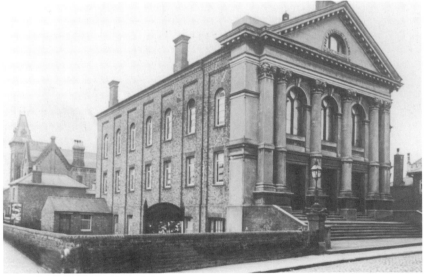

The United Methodist Church.
Looking down Spring Gardens on the
left can be seen in the distance the
Christian Association Rooms.
Photograph about 1900.

The building that was built for the Christian Association in 1875, now used as a fitness centre. Photographed 2001.

Situated immediately behind the church was a scrap yard belonging to J. T. White & Son Ltd., and next to this for some years was a small fish and chip shop. Both of these have gone, and the site is now a car park for the next building along Spring Gardens. This building built of red brick in the French Gothic style was opened in the year 1875 as the Christian Association and Literary Institute. When built it contained a lecture hall, reading and class rooms, with a library of 1,600 volumes, and a resident caretaker.

The Christian Association after many years closed through lack of use, and the building was sold to Geest Industries who opened it as a Social Club for their workers. After some years the building was again put up for sale, and today it is a health and fitness centre, trading under the title of The Fitness Company.

Sunday School Parade float outside the Christian Association rooms in Spring Gardens. About 1900.

The Post Office sorting office built on the site that was previously occupied by the United Free Methodist Church.

W. A. Jepson Ltd., builders merchants

This picture taken in 1938 shows the proprietor, and workforce of W. A. Jepson Ltd., builders merchants of 22 Spring Gardens. The picture shows Jepson's as a typical small family business of the time. Mr. William Abraham Jepson, son of the founder of the firm is here seated second from the left. He passed away in 1942, and the business passed to Dorothy his widow, seated on his left in the photograph. Mrs. Jepson later married Mr. H. R. Edwards of Derbyshire. The business continued to be run by Mrs. Edwards until her death in 1977, after which it was managed by trustees for Mr. Edwards and their daughter. In 1981 the business was taken over by a firm from Retford and this ended over 100 years of trading for the family business.

The scene outside Jepson's yard in Spring Gardens in the early 1900s.

Jim's Motor repairs. This is the building that was once Jepson's builders merchants. Photographed 1998.

Snowdrop Villa.

One of the first houses to be built in Spring Gardens was "Snowdrop Villa", and was built by Mr. Robert Smart. He grew and dealt in snowdrops, and sold the bulbs to chemists for medicinal purposes. From the profit he made out of these tiny bulbs he built his house, and called it Snowdrop Villa.

It appears from various directories that Spring Gardens, formerly Brett's Walk, had a beerhouse called the Bricklayers Arms. Morris's Directory of 1863 records Benjamin Rodgers as a butcher and beer retailer, as does Kelly's Directory of 1868. White's Directory of 1872 gives a Henry Gould of 17 Spring Gardens as having a beerhouse. In an extract from the Spalding Free Press on 19th February 1907 it was said that Benjamin Rodgers had at one time owned the Bricklayers Arms in Spring Gardens, so it is a fair assumption that the Bricklayers Arms was at 17 Spring Gardens.

Snowdrop Villa. Photographed 2001.

Trades and Professions in Spring Gardens in 1937

Allen & Co., builders, 20 Spring Gardens.

Atton Bros, stone masons, 23 Spring Gardens.

Bean, Chas. E., house decorator, 8 Spring Gardens.

Hewett, Gertrude M. (Miss), dressmaker, 25 Spring Gardens.

Izett, Josephine (Miss), preparatory school, Literary Institute, Spring Gardens.

Jepson, Wm. A. Ltd., builders' merchants, 22 Spring Gardens.

Manchester Unity of Oddfellows (Welland Lodge) (G. T. Allen, sec.) Spring Gardens.

Merryweather, J. T., builder, Spring Gardens.

Parker, Cyril, fried fish dealer, 39 Spring Gardens.

Perkins, Ada M. (Mrs.), dressmaker, 1 Spring Gardens.

Pretty, Walter, surveyor, 23 Spring Gardens.

Spalding Christian Association & Literary Institute (William Atton, sec.), Spring Gardens.

White, J. T. & Son, marine store dealers, Spring Gardens.

Winsover Road

Winsover or Windsover Road as it used to be spelt until the middle of the 19th century stretches from the Telephone Exchange to the junction with Hawthorn Bank. In the first half of the 20th century Winsover Road had a large variety of shops and businesses. Kelly's Directory of 1937 gives six butchers, four bakers and four grocers, besides many other trades and professions many of which could not be found in the road today.

The first large shop to open in Winsover Road was the Spalding Industrial Co-operative Society Ltd., who were grocers, bakers, butchers, boot and shoe retailers, and dealers in hardware. Besides this they were coal and coke merchants and dairymen. Today the Co-op still trades on the same site as it originally opened up on, although the earlier shop, which was built about 1900, was demolished some years ago, and the present much larger modern building replaces it.

View along Winsover Road looking towards town. About 1900.

The Co-op shops in Winsover Road. About 1900.

115

Crowd assembled outside the Co-op for the official opening.

Bates the Bakers.

The Bates bakery business was started by Henry Bates in Commercial Road in 1855. By the 1860s the business had moved to Winsover Road where it continued trading for over 100 years. The business ceased baking at the end of the Second World War, but continued in business selling pet foods etc. by the grandson of the founder.

Bates bakery shop situated in Winsover Road on the corner of Mill Lane. The tall bake-house chimney can be seen at the rear of the shop, and in the bottom right hand corner can be seen the railway lines passing down Mill Lane. Photograph about 1880.

116

Charles Stanton, Iron Founder.

There had been several iron foundries in Spalding during the second half of the 19th century.

The largest iron foundry in Spalding was run by Charles Stanton who occupied premises at 21 Winsover Road. He started his business around the beginning of the 20th century in premises that had previously been occupied by Shepherd's Brewery, The foundry also had an entrance in Mill Lane which was situated at the side of the premises. Supplies for the foundry would arrive by rail. A wagon turntable was situated on one of the railway sidings. This allowed trucks to be turned so that they could be pulled by horses along the railway lines that passed through Glenn Avenue, across Winsover Road, and into Mill Lane to the foundry entrance.

In 1908 Stanton's were given a contract to supply cast iron pipes for the Urban District Council's new water main to Bourne.

Stanton's has been closed down for many years, and since then there has been no iron foundry in Spalding.

Stanton's Iron Foundry on the corner of Mill Lane. The Aldi store now stands on the site where Mill Lane once was.

Horses pulling trucks across Winsover Road from the main line into Mill Lane. The foundry stopped using horses in the 1930s because in frosty weather the horses sometimes slipped, and this brought protests from members of the public.

More Aspects of Spalding

Glenn Avenue photographed in 1993 showing where the railway lines used to go.

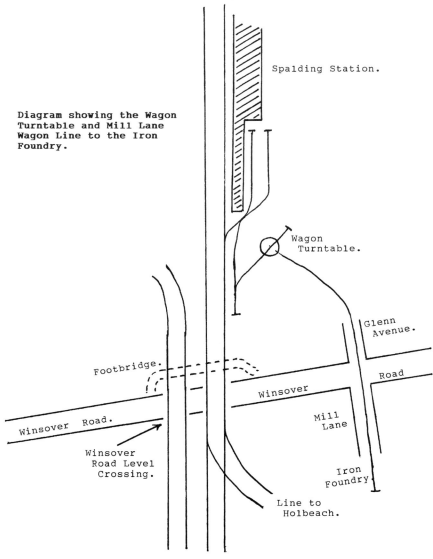

Diagram showing the Wagon Turntable and Mill Lane Wagon Line to the Iron Foundry.

Spalding Station.

Wagon Turntable.

Glenn Avenue.

Footbridge.

Winsover Road.

Winsover   Road

Mill Lane

Iron Foundry

Winsover Road Level Crossing.

Line to Holbeach.

118

Trades and Professions in Winsover Road in 1937.

Adams, George, pork butcher, 12 Winsover Road.

Aitken, Lucy (Miss), typewriting office, 190 Winsover Road.

Allen, Wm. Rt. & Sons, grocers, 77 Winsover Road.

Barrand, Betsy Ann (Mrs.) draper, 24 Winsover Road.

Basker, Jn. Wm., pork butcher, 4 Winsover Road.

Bates, Alfred, baker, 20 Winsover Road.

Bedford, Geo. Wm., confectioner, 22a Winsover Road.

Bennett, H. & Son., butchers, 128 Winsover Road.

Billett, Jn. Wm., grocer, 235 Winsover Road; fruiter, 236 Winsover Road.

Blackburn, E. & Sons., motor garage, Winsover Road.

Booth, Philip, fried fish dealer, 133 Winsover Road.

Boston Coal Co. Ltd., coal merchants, Station Gates, Winsover Road.

Boyd Ltd., piano dealer, 21 Winsover Road.

Campbell, Edward, fried fish dealer, 14 Winsover Road.

Carrington Haulage & Motor Co. Ltd., Winsover Road.

Cooper, F. & E. (Misses), confectioners, Winsover Road.

Cross, Elizabeth (Miss), confectioner, 15 Winsover Road.

Downs, John T., confectioner, 6 Winsover Road.

Elliott, Percy, dentist, 222 Winsover Road.

Emmitt, Fred, tailor, 128a Winsover Road.

Gibbons, J. W. & Son., cycle dealers, Winsover Road.

Goodey, Chas. H., butcher, 16 Winsover Road.

Gosling, E. & Sons, boot dealers, 221 Winsover Road.

Gow, Percy, beer retailer, 238 Winsover Road.

Gray, George H., plumber, 17 Winsover Road.

Ground, Kate (Mrs.), Railway Tavern, 23 Winsover Road.

Hancock, Edward A., coal & coke merchants, 239 Winsover Road.

Hardy, Alfred, baker, 33 Winsover Road.

Harrison, Harold S., drug store, 19 Winsover Road.

Hayes, Jacob, sign writer, 2 Winsover Road.

Healey, H. & Sons., bulb growers, 112 Winsover Road.

Johnson, P., bakers, 224 Winsover Road.

Moore, Charlotte (Mrs.), shopkeeper, 211 Winsover Road.

Moore, Herbert S., hairdresser, 226 Winsover Road.

Nelson, Harriet A. (Mrs.), wardrobe dealer, 38 Winsover Road.

Nelson, Hilda (Mrs.), 4a & 5 Winsover Road.

Northern Hotel (Horace Ernest Skipworth), 7 Winsover Road.

Owen, Jn., confectioner, 13 Winsover Road.

Parker, Herbert, shopkeeper, 11 Winsover Road.

Parkinson, Alfred, butcher, 22 & 194a Winsover Road.

Pepper, Ann Eliz. (Mrs.), dressmaker, 105 Winsover Road.

Perkins, J. R., coal agent, 76 Winsover Road.

Pied Bull Inn (Jn. Thos. Bloodworth), 121 Winsover Road.

Pocklington, M. & R., car dismantler, Glenn Avenue, Winsover Road.

Rayner, Jn. C., grocer, 27 Winsover Road.

Shelton, Maurice, boot repairer, Winsover Road.

Spalding Industrial Co-operative Society Ltd. grocers, bakers, butchers, boot & shoes, hardware, coal & coke merchants, dairymen &c. 231 Winsover Road.

Spalding Urban District Electricity Dept., 9 Winsover Road.
Stanton Charles, ironfounders, 21 Winsover Road.
Storr, W. E. & Sons, dairymen, 8 Winsover Road.
Tombling,. Wm. Rt., plumbers, 233 Winsover Road.
Tomlinson, Maud Mary (Mrs), shopkeeper, 204 Winsover Road.
Wheatman, Chas., carpenter, 218 Winsover Road.
Whitaker, A. S., motor body builder, Winsover Road.
Wilcox, Sydney, coal dealer, 187 Winsover Road.
Wilson, Ernest, electrical engineer, 10 Winsover Road.
Wingfield. Lily (Mrs.), confectioner, 26 Winsover Road.
Woollard, H. C. & Son., saddlers, 160 Winsover Road.
Wootton, Jsph. Wm., house decorator, 225 Winsover Road.
Wright, Fred, boot repairer, 144 Winsover Road.

Re *F. E. STEVENSON's ASSIGNMENT.*
SPALDING, Lincolnshire.
To *IRONFOUNDERS, IRONMONGERS, and Others.*
To be SOLD by AUCTION
(By direction of the Assignees),
By Mr. SAMUEL KINGSTON,
At the Red Lion Hotel, in Spalding, on Friday, July 23rd, 1897, at 3 for 4 o'clock in the Afternoon, subject to such conditions of sale as will then be declared.

ALL that MESSUAGE and IRONMONGER's SHOP, with the Ironfoundry, Two Blacksmiths' Shops, Fitting and Carpenters' Shops, Stable, Hayloft, and Outbuildings adjoining and belonging thereto; together with the TRAMWAY running from the Foundry to the Great Northern Railway and the Turntables and other conveniences attached thereto, situate on the Winsover-road, Spalding aforesaid, late in the occupation of the Executors of the late Mr. F. E. STEVENSON.

The Boiler, Steam Engine, and fixed Plant and Machinery in and about the Foundry are not included in the Sale, but the purchaser will have the option of purchasing the same at a Valuation to be made in the usual way.

An extensive Foundry Business has for many years been carried on upon the Premises, which are in immediate connection with the Great Northern, the Great Eastern, and Midland Lines of Railway, and the railway trucks or waggons can be loaded upon the premises and taken along the Tramway on to the several companies' systems.

The purchase is to be completed on the 11th October next, on which day possession will be given, but arrangements can be made for immediate possession if desired.

The whole or any part of the purchase-money can be had on approved security.

For further particulars and to view the premises apply to the Auctioneer; to Messrs. Poppleton and Appleby, chartered accountants, 164, Aldersgate-street, London, and 26, Corporation-street, Birmingham; to Mr. George Kingston, Spalding; or to
Messrs. H. H. and L. C. HARVEY,
10th July, 1897   Solicitors, Spalding.

Advertisement for the sale of the Iron Foundry in Winsover Road. July 1897. This was the foundry that was eventually taken over by Charles Stanton.

Edward Hancock, standing in the doorway of his shop in Winsover Road. Early 1900s.

View along Winsover Road looking towards town. The Pied Bull Inn is on the right. Photographed in the 1930s.

View looking along Winsover Road towards the town about 1920. In the right hand corner of the photograph is the baker's cart of J. C. Rayner's who had a bakery and grocery shop in Winsover Road for over fifty years.

High Street.

High Street runs north from the High Bridge, and ends close to where the old Albert Bridge used to stand. In its time this street has possessed some of the finest houses in the town, and also two large mills. The first of these was the South Holland Mill that for many years was owned by G. W. Plowman and Son. This mill has been closed down for some years, and has now been converted into living accommodation. The other mill was owned by G. F. Birch and Son Ltd., and this disappeared some years earlier.

Close to the High Bridge was the White Lion Hotel. This served as a hotel for over 150 years, but has now been transformed into living accommodation.

There is no doubt that the finest house would have been Holland House which had stabling and grounds that ran through to Halmer Gate where there was a Lodge House. Over the years this house was the home of several influential families who left their mark upon the town in various ways. The house was built in the 1760s to a design by the well known architect, William Sands, who was also responsible for several other properties in the town. The builders were George Andrew and John Sharpe.

In 1909 part of the stabling and much of the grounds to the rear of Holland House was sold for building purposes, and Holland Road was created which ran from High Street through to Halmer Gate.

In 1941 the house was purchased by the Spalding Urban District Council for £2,250. From 1942 until 1950 the Holland War Agricultural Executive Committee took over the house as offices.

In 1960 the remainder of the stabling, coach house and carriage entrance was demolished and new Government Offices were built on the corner of High Street and Holland Road.

For some years Holland House was partly used as an Unemployment Benefit Office, with some of the building being used by the Social Services Department of the Lincolnshire County Council, and a small office used by the Registrar of Births and Deaths.

On the 16th January, 1993, Holland House was severely damaged by fire. The fire was reported about 7 a.m. and within a short while up to twelve fire engines were on the scene. The fire which was reported to have started on the ground floor ravaged through the building and part of the roof collapsed.

For a long while the building remained boarded up and surrounded by scaffolding, but eventually the authorities had the building renovated, and it is now back in use as offices.

The White Lion Hotel in High Street, about 1950.

Holland House in High Street. About 1900.

The site that is now occupied by the Holland Road car park was where Elmsford House once stood. This house was built by Mr. Thomas Foster, an attorney, in 1797.

For several years this house was the home of the Maples family.

Kelly's Directory of Lincolnshire for 1933 gives Elmsford House as the home of the Spalding and District Labour Club and Institute Ltd. Their secretary at that time was A. P. Palmer.

Further along High Street from Elmsford House is Yew Lodge, a fine three storey house built by Mr. Henry Everard about 1760, and is still used as a home.

Elmsford House when the Labour Club occupied the premises. Photographed 1932.

Yew Lodge. Photographed 2001.

Next to Yew Lodge is the Cley Hall Hotel. This was built as a house in 1754 by Mr. Theophilus Buckworth who was lord of the manor of Spalding cum Croyland. Theophilus married a Miss Cley, and named the house after her family. Their daughter Ann Elizabeth in 1787 married Maurice, the eldest son of Colonel Johnson of Ayscoughfee Hall. Eventually the house passed to his grandson, Theophilus Fairfax Johnson, who left Cley Hall in 1841 to live in Holland House. His son Theophilus Maurice Stephen Johnson continued living at Cley Hall until the death of his father in 1853 when he then took up residence in Holland House.

Cley Hall Hotel.
Photographed 2001.

Townscape

Opposite Birch's Mill, on the side of the river, once stood a large narrow wooden warehouse belonging to the mill. This was used in the days when the port was in use. Birch's were the last people to bring their barges upstream to unload in the late 1930s.

Looking upstream from the Albert Bridge in June 1923. Birch's warehouse can be seen in this photograph on the river side.

The blacksmith's forge in High Street. Photographed in 1973. The white building next door was once occupied by a sail maker when the port was in use. Later this became a fish and chip shop, but today it has been converted into living accommodation.

Also on the side of the river is the blacksmith's forge that has been in the Dodd's family for many years. The present owner is Mr. Geof Dodd who is well known for his long involvement with the building of the floats for the Spalding Flower Parade.

Geof's father Mr. Jim Dodd was the last person to hold the post of Harbour Master, and one of his tasks was to open the old Albert Bridge that crossed the river close to their forge, when shipping needed to pass.

Trades and Professions in High Street in 1937.

Adams, George, fruiters, 2a High Street.
Birch, G. F. & Son Ltd., straw merchants, High Street.
Dodd, Geo, blacksmith & harbour master, High Street.
Garwell, Ernest Jn. corn & flour merchants, 1 High Street.
Groom, W. Ltd., timber merchants, South Holland Saw Mills, High Street.
Hills, Jn. Rd., insurance agent, 28 High Street.
Holland County Council Education Committee, Holland House, High Street.
Munro, James Ramsey, M.D., surgery, High Street.
Parsons, Jn. & Son., plumbers, 6 High Street.
Plowman, G. W. & Son., millers, High Street.
Spalding Egg Packers Ltd., High Street.
Spalding Industrial Co-operative Society Ltd., 34 High Street.
Wass, Geo. Hy., fruit grower, Linden House, High Street.
White Lion Hotel (Mark Thorpe proprietor), High Street.
Worley, Wm., fried fish dealer, 41 High Street.

Private Residents.

Birch, Geo. Fras., Cley Hall, High Street.
Bulmer, John Henry, 24 High Street.
Elsom, George, 9 High Street.
Frost, Herbert George, J. P., Holland House, High Street.
Gleed, John W., M.A., D.L., J.P., West Elloe, High Street.
Luck, Harry, 18 High Street.
Maples, Miss E. M., 10 High Street.
Munro, James Ramsey, M.D., High Street.
Plowman, George Wm. Selby House, High Street.
Sly, Mrs. 11, High Street.
Sutcliffe, J., 12 High Street.
Tointon, Samuel, Yew House, High Street.

Stonegate.

The course that Stonegate takes is a very ancient track that could possibly go back to the time of the Romans. It was not until the last few years of the 19th century that houses started to be built along the road that was formerly called Spalding Drove.

As you entered Stonegate, on the left there used to be a Tithe Barn. A pair of police houses were built on this site for the Holland County Police in the 1930s. Next to these standing back from the road are a pair of very old houses. Miss D. Izett who was at one time headmistress of the Westlode Street School once lived in one of these, and said that when she first came to Spalding, Stonegate was only a narrow path.

Pair of Houses at the top of Stonegate, Numbers 96 and 97. The date that these were built is unknown, but could well be late 18th or early 19th century.

On the right hand side as you enter the road are a row of three cottages that were built in 1795. These cottages appear to have been built around the same time as the large house that stands behind them. This house although now officially classed as being in Love Lane was called and still is known as Stonegate Lodge. It was built by Samuel Dinham a Solicitor who lived there until he died in 1829.

The oldest house that stood in Stonegate was "Halmer Grange" a farmhouse that was demolished to make room for the building of the Spalding High School for Girls. It is thought that the name "Halmer" comes from a Norman knight called Richard D'Almere who had associations with this area. Replace the D with H and you get "Halmere" or "Halmer".

Nos 1, 2 and 3. Stonegate. These cottages were built in 1795.
Photographed here in 1972 before they underwent restoration.

In the 19th century the Rev. Dr. William Moore's coachman named John Wilson lived in this house being little more than a stone's throw from the church.

A man named Williams followed Wilson into Halmer Grange, and he went as coachman to Mr. T. M. S. Johnson of Holland House.

The last person to live in Halmer Grange was Mr. Noah Bates and his family who moved in during the 1880s living there and working the farm for over 70 years.

Halmer Grange, Stonegate. Photographed 1926.

Stonegate in 1997 showing the view where Halmer Grange once stood. The High School is to the right out of the picture.

Halmer Grange, Stonegate. The rear view in 1890. Left to right: Mr. Noah Bates (Snr.), Cissie Bates (daughter), Louie Bates, Mrs. Noah Bates, Eddie (almost out of sight), Noah (son), Hannah, Harold (on horse), Stanley (with goat).

In 1938 the Holland Education Committee made a resolution to negotiate the purchase of Halmer Grange with its 8½ acres of land from Mr. Noah Bates for the purpose of building a new High School for Girls. This resolution was put on hold due to the start of the Second World War. Eventually in 1944 the property was purchased, but it was not vacated until the 1950s.

Halmer Grange was demolished, and in February 1957 the foundations were prepared for the building of the new school which was intended to be completed for the Autumn Term in 1958. This was over ambitious, and the new school eventually began on Thursday 8th January, 1959 when 300 girls were housed in the school while 70 girls still remained at the old school in London Road.

On Friday 20th March 1959 the school was officially opened by Sir Herbert Butcher, M.P. for Holland with Boston. Since the school was opened there have been several large additions to the buildings, and all the pupils are now housed in the one complex.

During the Second World War, Stonegate was bombed in an air raid in May 1941. The raid took place in the early morning when the first three bombs fell harmlessly in Mr. Noah Bates' field close to Halmer Grange. These were uncomfortably near dwelling houses to which considerable damage was caused. One of the three bombs fell only fifteen feet from an underground shelter in which a number of people were accommodated. A fourth bomb fell on a concrete path in the front garden of 68 Stonegate where a lady was killed, and a man seriously injured, although he recovered after several weeks in the Johnson Hospital. Also in number 68 was a lady and her daughter from neighbouring house number 66. The lady who was 74 received injuries from which she died later in hospital, but the daughter was only slightly injured. At the time the bomb fell all four were in the front room. The house was damaged at the front, and scores of other houses in the vicinity had windows and doors shattered, and ceilings fell down.

In the same raid a bungalow in neighbouring Alexandra road received a hit which completely demolished it. The occupants had a miraculous escape when they were rescued unhurt from under the roof which had collapsed upon them as they lay in bed.

Spalding High School for Girls. Photographed 2001.

Trades and Professions in Stonegate in 1937.

Arnold, Cyril M., coal merchant, 30 Stonegate.
Ashton, Wm. Edwd., supt. of the South Holland Drainage, 82 Stonegate.
Barnett, Thos., bulb grower, Stonegate.
Bates Bros., farmers, 77 Stonegate.
Cocking, Benj. S., insurance agent, 52 Stonegate.
Cole, Owen Rees, grocers & sub post office, 62 Stonegate.
Gibbs, Sidney, boot and shoe repairer, 89 Stonegate.
Golding, Florence (Mrs), boarding house keeper, 49 Stonegate.
Holding, T. H. & Son, potato merchant, 5 Stonegate.

HALMER GRANGE, SPALDING.
202 *SHEEP*, 14 *BEASTS*, 4 *HORSES*, *IMPLEMENTS*, and *Effects*.

S. and G. KINGSTON will SELL, upon the premises of Mr. JOHN WILLSON, Halmer Grange, Spalding, on Monday, March 22d, 1880, the following Live and Dead Farming STOCK and Effects, comprising 202 SHEEP, viz., 128 lamb hogs, 72 in lamb ewes, 2 shearling long-wool rams; 14 BEASTS, viz., 13 $1\frac{1}{2}$-year-old steers and heifers and a yearling bull; 4 HORSES, viz., black horse (Farmer) 7 years, black horse (Short) 9 years, brown nag mare (Kitty) 7 years, quiet to ride and drive; a half-bred yearling colt by Sampson the 2d ; the Agricultural IMPLEMENTS, Cart and Plough Gears, &c.

The Live Stock will be found in good condition and well deserving the attention of purchasers.

The Sale is in consequence of Mr. Willson quitting.

The whole will be sold strictly for ready money, and without the slightest reserve, commencing with the Implements at 2 o'clock in the Afternoon to a minute.

Advert for a farm sale at Halmer Grange, March 22nd, 1880.

Snippets from what the Papers used to say

July 1858

CRICKET: – The All-England eleven match commences on Thursday next, and should the weather be fine, it will doubtless prove very attractive. The field (in Love Lane) is very picturesque, and being so near to the town, affords every convenience for witnessing the game.

SERIOUS LOSS: – On Wednesday last, an industrious young man, late in the service of F. Millns, Esq., had the misfortune to lose a valuable sow. She is supposed to have been poisoned. Unfortunately, the young man has a large family and a bedridden wife. This case appears deserving the assistance of our charitable friends.

ACCIDENT: – On Thursday morning, a portion of the beast market, formerly the old Westlode, an open sewer that used to flow the whole length of the road and empty itself into the river Welland, near to Carter's brewery, and which had been arched over, suddenly gave way, but we are happy to say nothing happened. We hope that our Commissioners will now have the whole of it examined and repaired if necessary, so as to prevent any further accidents.

September 1858

WATER: – The want of this great necessary of life is most severely felt in this town every summer, but seldom more severely than this year. Now that an Artesian well has been opened at Bourne, of such power and capacity as to be able to supply not only that town but Spalding and Boston also with an adequate supply of the pure and beautiful element of water, this certainly seems to be the time, if ever, when a feasible scheme for the establishment of a Water Works Company could be carried out. The subject has often been brought before the public, but has always been abandoned, principally because a sufficient supply of water could not be insured. This new well at Bourne, however, gives out with great power water at the rate of upwards of 190 million gallons per annum. Here then is a supply which in all probability will be unfailing, and it only remains now for some public benefactor to devise and mature a plan for conveying the water here, and by so doing confer the greatest boon which Spalding could receive.

THE COMET: – This astronomical visitor is visible nearly every evening, and was especially so on Thursday evening, the atmosphere being clear, the nucleus was very brilliant.

October 1858

PADDLE PLEASURE BOAT: – A very pretty pleasure boat was launched on Tuesday week, and was an object of great curiosity. It has been built by Mr. West, painter, and is propelled by paddles similar to a steamer, worked by two persons.

THE FIRE BRIGADE: – At the meeting of the Improvement Commissioners on Friday last, a new fire brigade was formed, the old one being broken up in consequence of a disagreement between the men and the superintendent, who being "an old soldier", was desirous of introducing a mode of discipline calculated to awaken the latent energies of the brigade and quicken their operations in cases of fire. The men, however, had been accustomed to take matters very easy on practice days, and if no great defects were found in the engines, &c., were content to pack all up again without going through the various evolutions sought to be introduced by the present superintendent; they therefore broke out into open mutiny, disobeyed his word of command, and many of the corps sent in their resignation to the commissioners, who considered there was no sufficient ground of complaint against the superintendent, and that his proposed practice was calculated to improve the efficiency of the brigade. The resignations were accordingly accepted, and notices issued for the formation of a new brigade, the members of the old one being eligible for re-election.

SPALDING: – Night Jury; On Wednesday night last, some of these gentry amused themselves by daubing the windows and shutters of their more respectable neighbours with sewer dirt. Some of the parties were seen at their pranks and have been cautioned.

November 1858

DIPTHERIA: – The painful and dangerous disease has carried off many victims during the last three months, and is still very prevalent here and at Pinchbeck, one medical man alone assured us he has twelve patients in the town and neighbourhood. It is chiefly fatal with children and young people. Where gargles and other inward applications can be used constantly, the disease is soon overcome, especially when medical aid is sought early.

PENNY BANKS: – J. Hopkins, Esq., has set foot a scheme for the establishment of a penny bank, for the benefit of the working classes, &c., of this town and neighbourhood; they are useful auxiliaries to the Government Savings Banks and we wish it success.

December 1858

THE LAST COACH: – On the 20th ult., the Royal Mail Coach, the last of the old stagers in this neighbourhood took its final journey from the White Hart, being knocked off the road by the Holbeach railway.

BUTTER MARKET: – The Improvement Commissioners are inviting tenders to be sent in before their monthly meeting on Friday next, from persons willing to contract for the tolls payable by the sellers of poultry, butter, &c., on market days. The tolls for the year ending 25th September last produced £13.16s.11d.

January 1859

FIRE: – Between five and six o'clock on Thursday morning last, the inhabitants were against startled by the cry of "fire" and it was discovered that the house occupied by Wm. Mason, basket maker, on the New Road, was enveloped in flames, and from the very inflammable nature of the stock-in-trade and materials the fire spread with great rapidity – in fact it had got so strong a hold before it was discovered that escape by the staircase being cut off the inmates were let out of the windows, and saved nothing but their night clothes. The engines were speedily on the spot, but the supply of water was so short that they could render but little service, and the house and stock was completely destroyed; the adjoining house was in considerable danger for some time, and the furniture was removed, but beyond some glass being broken by the heat no great damage was done. The house belonging to Mr. Henry Brigg, Esq., and was one of the few old thatched houses remaining in Spalding, and formed part of the "Punch Bowl" Inn property. It is supposed that the fire originated in the cellar, which was used as a workshop, but the cause appears wrapped in mystery. Mason was insured to the amount of £150.

February 1859

THE GENTLEMEN'S SOCIETY: – The members of this ancient society held a meeting on the 7th instant. The Rev. J. H. Marsden, B.D., Professor of Archaeology to the University of Cambridge, presided. Several objects of an antiquarian interest were exhibited, and a paper of the nomenclature of the towns and villages of this country, was read by the Rev. Robert Hollis, of Spalding.

ACCIDENT: – An old man named Thomas Boor, overlooker of the corn mill in the Workhouse, met with an accident whilst working the mill on Saturday week, by which he lost two fingers and a part of a thumb, these members having become entangled in a part of the machinery and crushed so severely that Dr. Morris found it necessary to resort to amputation.

SHOCKING DEATH: – On Saturday morning the body of a woman named Davidson was found in the river Welland, near to the Crane Inn, Double Street. Late on Friday night she was seen in Herring Lane, going towards the river, and somewhat worse for drink, which was, unfortunately, too often the case: and it is supposed she walked across the road instead of turning to the right or left, and fell into the river from the quay. An inquest was held before W. Edwards, Esq., coroner, at the Crane Inn, and a verdict of "Found drowned" was returned.

April 1859

HORSE SHOW: – The first show of entire horses was held on Tuesday last, and was tolerably large for the first day. Whilst the horses were running the notorious Jerry Hickling struck one of them with his stick, and received a severe kick in return, which knocked him down but did him no serious injury.

FIRE: – An alarm of fire was raised on Wednesday afternoon about 4 o'clock, the roof of a workshop on the foundry premises of Mr. C. D. Jennings having become ignited. The engines were called out, but they were scarcely required, as the fire was discovered when plenty of help was at hand, and it was soon extinguished without much damage being done.

August 1859

PRESENTATION: – A very costly lectern has been lately placed in the parish church. It is manufactured of brass, and is in the form of an eagle with expanded wings, mounted upon a massive brass pedestal. This handsome ornament is the gift of T. M. S. Johnson Esq., and forms a conspicuous object in the centre aisle – hardly in keeping however with the high old fashioned pews. The lectern was formerly used in most churches, the lessons for the day being read therefrom, but it has generally been superseded by the reading desk, as was the case here, until about twelve months ago, when a substantial oak lectern was provided, which continued in use until the introduction of the present one.

ACCIDENT: – Horse dealers as a class are proverbially reckless amongst the animals with which they have most to do: whipping, spurring, and shouting in such a manner that it is a matter of surprise that many accidents do not happen in horse fairs. On Monday, a man on horseback suddenly put spurs to his horse, causing it to kick most violently amongst a crowd of bystanders. One man was very much hurt by this unnecessary and untimely use of the spur; the horse kicked him, it is said, two or three times before he could be got out of the way, when he was quite insensible, and, upon arrival of medical aid, it was found that his collar-bone and one or two ribs were broken, and some other injuries sustained.

RIOTS: – On Tuesday, several disgraceful drunken rows took place here, and in the evening one of the parties was dragged to the police station in a heavy state of intoxication, and locked up for the night.

THE FAIR: – The August fair, on Monday last, was attended by many buyers; but the show of horses and stock of all kinds was very small, and the prices were generally lower than at the June fair.

NUISANCE: – The attention of the Improvement Commissioners has very properly been drawn to the state of some-slaughter-houses near to the railway-station. The stench from these places has long been a subject of great annoyance and complaint, not only to the inhabitants in the neighbourhood, but also to strangers arriving by rail. It is a matter of some difficulty to deal with, for these places must be somewhere – on the other hand the health of many must be looked after and ensured even at the cost and inconvenience of the few. The most effectual mode of getting rid of the nuisance would be for the Improvement Commissioners to erect slaughter-houses at a convenient distance from the town and let them to the butchers, or charge the butchers so much per head for each animal slaughtered: under a proper officer this plan would overcome all difficulties, would be a convenience than not to the trade, and might, by the sale of the sewage and manure &c., become a source of profit as well as a sanitary benefit to the rate payers.

September 1859

NARROW ESCAPE: – Mr. H. T. Stiles, surgeon, narrowly escaped being killed on Thursday night. He, accompanied with a lady, was driving through the Market-place, when, a child being in the road, he pulled up suddenly, and was, with the lady, thrown out of the gig, but neither of them was seriously injured.

THE CHURCH: – An apparatus for the warming of the interior of the church is about to be introduced. It is of an effective character it will be a great addition to the comfort of the churchgoers, for during the winter the sacred edifice is far too cold for persons of delicate constitutions to venture to.

EARLY CLOSING: – We hear that the shops of the principal trades in the town will close at seven o'clock in the evening from the first week in October until April. This has become a custom for some trades, but this year, we are informed, it will be more extensive than ever.

INDEPENDENT CHAPEL: – A fine harmonium has been placed in this chapel, and was played on Sunday for the first time, causing a great improvement in the singing part of the service. The Rev. Percy Strutt preached the anniversary sermons in aid of the Sunday Schools in connection with the chapel, and liberal donations were made in furtherance of the cause.

October 1859

A RUNAWAY: – On Wednesday morning a horse, attached to a cart, both belonging to Mr. Brett, builder, started at full gallop from the spring close up the lake behind the Welland Terrace, and along the London road, through the railway gates, luckily without meeting anything on the road; just through the gates it ran foul of a lamp-post, breaking it and the cart and harness, when the horse being free stood perfectly quiet and still.

NEW CLOCK: – For some months past speculation has been rife as to the motive for fixing a large clock dial in front of the gaol with hands always pointing at 12.45; the mystery is now cleared up, the said dial having been made to determine the proper size for a permanent one. The name of the donor of the new clock was for some time a secret, it is not so now, for the clock came down from London and was marking the time in Mr. Preston's shop on Saturday last, the inner dial bearing the following inscription: "Presented by the Rev. Dr. Moore, D.D., Chairman of the Spalding Quarter Sessions, A.D. 1859."

HOUSE FALLING: – An old dilapidated house, next to the Corn Exchange, in the Market-place, partly fell in on Saturday last. When the site for the Exchange was decided upon, it was thought it desirable to have this house included therein; but the owner set such an extravagant price upon the place, that the Improvement Commissioners were obliged to do without it; and although they offered Mr. Mounteney a larger and better house close by (which has since been pulled down), and a certain sum of money besides, he decided upon sticking to the old shop.

NARROW ESCAPE: – During the market on Tuesday, a piece of slate was dropped by some men at work on the Exchange, upon the glass roof of the Butter-market; and; although the market was just at its height, luckily no one was in the way of the broken glass &c., or they might have been injured.

THE RIFLE CORPS: – We are glad to find that some active steps are being taken towards the formation of a corps of Volunteer Rifles in this town; upwards of thirty names have been sent in, and now the Government has increased the allowance of arms and ammunition from 25 to 50 per cent, there can be no difficulty in a neighbourhood like this in raising a sufficient sum to supply the volunteers with the remaining half required.

November 1859

FIRE: – An alarm of fire was raised on Monday morning in Little London, but, fortunately, it was extinguished before much harm was done, and although the engines were taken to the scene of disaster they were not required, as the fire had been got under by the efforts of some persons on the spot.

FIFTH OF NOVEMBER: – Guy Fawkes Day passed over very quietly this year; in fact, now that the observance of the day by Church services is abolished by the Act of Parliament which was passed in March last, we have not even the church bells chiming to remind us of the celebrated Gunpowder Plot.

ODD FELLOWS: – Last Friday evening the anniversary of the "Perseverance Lodge" of Odd Fellows (MU) was celebrated at the large room of the Black Bull Inn (Host Metherell's). A splendid supper was enjoyed at 7 o'clock, after which E. Morris, Esq., M.D. took the chair, when the usual loyal and patriotic toasts followed, the attendance being highly respectable. The affairs of the lodge are reported to be in a very successful and improving state.

December 1859

SPALDING: – The fat stock fair on Tuesday may only be considered large as regards the beasts, of which there was a greater number than usual, and some of very superior quality. Good stock was bought readily, and as much as 8s. and 9s. per stone was obtained in several cases. Upwards of a dozen very fine oxen, fed by Mr. Thomas Plowright, jun., were sold at £41 per head. There was only a small supply of sheep, and very few horses were offered for sale.

CHRISTMAS: – If Monday 26th instant is not a universal holiday here, it will, at least, be a general one amongst the trade establishments; the drapers having set the example announcing by handbills their intention of closing their shops the day after Christmas day. It is hoped other employers will also extend the festive holiday of the season to a similar length, and that all who are able may spend a merry Christmas.

THE GENERAL BAPTISTS: – Perhaps no dissenting congregation has increased in this town to such an extent as the General Baptists. It is not many years ago since their chapel was considerably enlarged, and now it is again found necessary to extend it so as to provide for the still increasing congregation.

SKATING: – A match was run last Monday, over a course marked out on the river Welland, from the Queens Head Inn nearly to the Lock's Mill, twice round. The Crowlanders maintained their fame on this occasion, a man named Sharp from that place carrying off the money (about £5).

January 1860

SHEEP STEALING: – Last Saturday night, a sheep, the property of Mr. T. Plowright, was slaughtered in a field in Clay Lake, and the best part of the carcass carried away.

SOUTH HOLLAND RIFLE CORPS: – The members of the South Holland division, to the number of about 30, met in the large room at the New Bell Inn, on Tuesday evening, for a preliminary drill; a sergeant of the 21st gave the volunteers some active exercise for about two hours, and announced that he would be in attendance the next evening for a similar parade. The room is not nearly large enough for the purpose, but has been taken until the Improvement Commissioners reply to the application for the Exchange Hall, they having agreed to let it to the Rifle Corps on the same terms as other town bodies.

PIGEON SHOOTING: – A match for £20 came off yesterday (Thursday) week, between Sheriff Blades of this town, and Mr. Harris, of London. Blades was the winner, shooting in good style fourteen birds out of nineteen. Harris shot eleven out of eighteen. We hear that Harris is the same party who beat the celebrated American pigeon shooter, King, a few weeks ago.

February 1860

ACCIDENTS: – On Tuesday evening, the horse engaged in collecting the stalls after market, ran away with part of its load, and one of the stalls, coming in contact with the lamp post opposite Mr. G. C. Osborn's struck the name plate at the bottom of his window, which was much broken; the plate glass window however escaped, although the blow was given within six inches of it. – During Mr. S. Kingston's horse sale on Tuesday, owing to the very dangerous state of the New Road, which was then covered with ice, one of the animals slipped up, and fell heavily on its side. – The same evening, an elderly female slipped, and fell in the Market Place, and was much shaken.

ALARM OF FIRE: – Just as the attendants at the ball were closing the Corn Exchange, on Saturday morning, an alarm of fire was given, and the hearth stone in the late newsroom being taken up, it was found that it had been laid upon the flood boards; the stone was a very thin one, and a large fire having been in the grate for some hours, the boards underneath had become gradually heated until they ignited. It would be a curious enquiry to find where the fault of this dangerous method of building lay, but as such inquiry would probably end in smoke as the above fire did luckily, it would be hardly advisable perhaps to provoke it. Surely the fire grates in other parts of the building are not set in a similar fashion.

HURRICANE: – Last Sunday afternoon, a terrific gale passed over this town, causing many accidents, but happily unattended with loss of life or limb. The first part of the gale came about three o'clock, and although this was by far the most severe, it continued only a short time. After an interval of about three quarters of an hour, during which time the wind was very high, accompanied by snow and rain, another hurricane came on, which lasted twenty minutes or half an hour, blowing with great force from north-west and south-west. The principal casualty is the falling of Mr. Kelk's steam mill chimney in Crackpool Lane. This structure has been considered somewhat unsafe for several years, and trial on Sunday's gale was more than it could bear: about thirty-six feet of the chimney shaft was broken off, falling upon a stable in the mill yard – a considerable quantity of the debris actually falling between two horses, one of which escaped unhurt, and the other with a slight scratch on the head. A portion of the roof of the Bull Inn (Mr. Palling's), was blown off, but the damage done was not great. On Mr. James Watson's property, on the Bourne Road, a chimney was blown down, smashing the roof of an outhouse on which it fell, doing considerable damage. Here a tree was also torn up by the roots, and a chimney pot and several slates were blown away. A large tree was also uprooted near the Red House, completely barricading the Low Road for some time; in fact, the fall of chimney pots, tiles and slates, and the overthrow of stacks, trees and barns, are innumerable.

March 1860

THE MARTS: – The principal mart day on Tuesday last brought a considerable number of visitors into the town, some of whom could have been very well spared, for their light fingers found their way into the pockets of several respectable persons, this person commencing so early as Monday night by way of proclamation probably. Manders menagerie was the chief attraction, and is really a good collection of specimens of natural history from all parts of the world; the band is an excellent one rivalling the celebrated Wombwell's. Cantrell's bazaar and a few peep shows comprised the remainder of the attractions.

THE CEMETERY: – The late gale did great damage to the cemetery chapels, blowing both the bells down, which falling upon the roofs, broke an immense quantity of slates, &c.; altogether the repairs will cost a sum approaching £100. Tenders are invited for the slating.

ACCIDENT: – Mr. Lavender, tailor, met with a severe accident on Saturday last, being gored and run over by a beast; up to Tuesday, his life was despaired of, but on Wednesday, he was considered out of danger.

April 1860

ACCIDENT: – on Saturday afternoon, Mr. Thomas Taylor, of the Oat Sheaf, in turning the corner from the Bourne Road into Thomazin Lane with a horse and cart, accidentally came into collision with the gig of Dr. Cammack, who was proceeding therein in a contrary direction. Taylor was not driving very fast, but still so much faster than the worthy Dr. that the concussion was great enough to break off the axle tree of the gig, and, in fact, to make such a complete wreck of the vehicle that the wonder is how the Dr. and his man and horse escaped with a few slight bruises only.

GROSS CRUELTY: – The woman Pennington who was apprehended, and brought before the magistrates, at the petty sessions, on Tuesday last, for pumping upon her child, aged about seven years, was dismissed with a most severe reprimand, which we hope will prevent a repetition of the inhuman treatment to which she has largely subjected her daughter.

May 1860

IMPROVEMENT COMMISSIONERS: – At the adjourned meeting held on Friday last, Mr. W. Pike took the oath and his seat on the board. The application of H. Hawkes, Esq., for leave to make a tramway across the Bourne Road from his steam flour mill to a siding of the Great Northern Railway, was postponed until the regular monthly meeting of the board. An improvement rate of 2s. in the pound was laid, according to the Act of Parliament. It was stated that, in addition to the sinking fund of £250 per annum, about £200 had ben paid off the loan. The estimates for the Town and Rural District Highway Rates were laid before the board; and after some discussion, a rural rate of 7d. in the pound was laid, and a town rate of 8d. in the pound for the repairs of the highway.

THE ROOK NUISANCE: – We regret to have to complain of the nuisance of the above birds in a much frequented part of our town, by their being permitted to build their nests and perch upon the branches of the trees above the pavement, which is not fit even to walk upon at this season of the year; we therefore hope now the rifles have arrived that one of the most energetic of our sergeants will drill (a hole through) the above birds, and thus get rid of the nuisance which ought not to exist in such a part. We remember an instance not long ago where the ivy was not allowed to hang over the top of the wall by the side of the footpath, and yet the trees alluded to are permitted to meet others on the opposite side of the road, so that there is no escape from the dirt, large drops of rain, &c., while walking beneath them.

POCKET PICKING: – The Chief Constable (Mr. C. Dolby) had his pocket picked last week when at the railway station en route for Boston Fair. A bridegroom was also eased of his purse whilst traveling in the train between here and Algarkirke station.

June 1860

MEAT STEALING: – On Saturday night, a woman was taken into custody for stealing a piece of meat off a butcher's stall in the Market Place. This practice is becoming very prevalent, and the unguarded way in which some of the stands are left is likely to encourage it.

ACCIDENT: – As Mr. E. Gooch and Mr. Tonge were proceeding to Donington fair last week, the horse they were driving stumbled and fell, throwing them both out of the cart; Mr. Tonge was much shaken, and when brought home by Mr. S. Kingston in the evening it was discovered that two ribs were broken. He is now going on favourably. Mr. Gooch was not hurt, but the mare's knees are very badly cut.

THE CRANE: – The crane upon the wharf in Double Street fell the other week before the potent power of the auctioneer's hammer, and was taken down and removed by the purchaser, Mr. Thos. Barwell, a few days ago: it had been rather out of repair for some time past – more from disuse, probably, than from overwork of late years – and was the last remaining relic of the "good old times" upon the river, having cleared many a ship of her cargo of merchandise before the railway turned the tide of traffic upon the swifter and surer iron road. The crane was erected about the year 1830.

STOCK FAIR: – The Stock Fair on Friday last was well supplied with both horses and beast, but the sale of them was very slow, prices being exceedingly high, and especially for fat beast, some being sold at a price which was estimated at 10s. per stone of 14 lbs. The horses were fresh, and the few which changed hands made great prices. There were but few sheep in the fair, but it may be mentioned that a bargain was made for a number of fat lambs to be delivered weekly to a butcher in the town to be paid for by weight at 9d. per lb.

CLUB FEAST: – The Oddfellows held their annual feast at the New Bell Inn, on Wednesday last; Dixon's band, which shows signs of great improvement; was in attendance to help on the pleasures of the day.

FIREWORKS: – Mr Gyngell, the pyrotechnist, paid us a visit here on Friday last, and exhibited some very excellent fireworks in the Market Place. The evening was tolerably well-suited for the display, and the company was numerous, but, we understand not very liberal.

CRUELTY TO ANIMALS: – An act of gross cruelty was committed by some young fellows last week upon a dog belonging to Mr. George Jones. The torture inflicted upon it by the application of turpentine to a most tender part drove the poor animal mad, and death put an end to its sufferings. A public prosecution would be proper punishment for the perpetrators; but, for the sake of their friends, and in hope of a thorough reformation in themselves, they have been let off on payment of £3 to the Blue Coat Charity and £2 to Mr. Jones.

July 1860

BLINKHORN AND COMPANY'S FIRE ENGINE AND FORCE PUMP: – On Monday, Superintendent Buffham, of the Spalding Fire Brigade, held the customary quarterly practice with the town fire engine, and consequently, Messrs. Blinkhorn availing themselves of the opportunity of trying their small engine side by side with the old-fashioned ones went down with the brigade to Mr. Tingey's field, where the several engines were put upon their trial – in each case, Messrs. Blinkhorns engine sent the greatest volume of water, both higher and further than either of the others. In filling a tank, which the other engine endeavoured to empty, the "Little Wonder", fully sustained its character, for although only a small portable engine capable of being taken into a room, and only worked by six men, it gained water by about 4 inches per minute on the brigade engine, which was vigorously handled by fourteen men.

"STOPPED UP": – The public have been put to great inconvenience for some weeks past owing to the stoppage of the Sheep market – the great highway to the Railway Station – which is being paved with granite, and this inconvenience is most shamefully continued, and without the least necessity, day after day. The whole of the immense traffic to and from the station has to pass through Deadman's Lane, where in some parts there is scarcely room for two vehicles to pass, and yet for all this scarcely a dozen yards of the new pavement were laid during last week, and on Tuesday nothing was done to forward the work, which then wanted but some score yards to complete it. In many towns this state of things would not be tolerated. What are the Commissioners or the Surveyor about?

SCHOOL FEAST: – The annual feast to the Church Sunday School children was held on Thursday, and was attended by a great number of visitors, who enjoyed themselves with dancing and other amusements. The Boston Band was in attendance.

FOOTBALL MATCH: – For a number of years the day after the school feast has been observed amongst the youth and manhood of the town almost as a general holiday, for upon the invitation of the Rev. Dr. Moore, they met annually in his paddock, and engaged in a hearty friendly game at football. This year the attendance was large, and seven good games were played.

CHEAP TRAINS: – A cheap special train from London on Saturday last brought several parties down on a short visit. An excursion to London is announced for the 6th August; another from Boston, if not from this station to Chatsworth and Matlock, on the 3rd August, and another on the 30th inst. to Hull.

August 1860

SOUP KITCHENS: – A notice has been issued by the acting town husbands, Robert Everard and William Edwards, Esq., calling a public meeting at the Exchange on Thursday next, for the purpose of establishing soup kitchens to aid the poor during the coming winter. We hope that the public will give their best aid to the furtherance of so charitable an object.

ACCIDENT: – On Friday last, a cart belonging to Mr. Walpole, of Pinchbeck, was accidentally forced into the window of Mr. Briggs, jeweller, by a wagon of Mr. John Caulton's breaking a large square of plate glass, and doing considerable damage to the stock. The cart was standing in Bridge Street, which is rather narrow, but there was plenty of room for the wagon to pass had the driver of it used proper care.

A DESERTER: – A severe chase was given to the officers of justice on Saturday, by a man who had deserted from the South Lincolnshire Militia. He came from Bourne that morning with his wife and child, and immediately on his arrival was taken into custody by the police. He managed, however, to give them the slip, and making for the cricket field scaled the wall into Mr. Metherell's late premises, and so on into Pinchbeck Street, through Elsom's rope walk, and over the surrounding fields. After a run of some three hours he was at length captured by Sergeant Fry of the 21st.

NARROW ESCAPE: – On Saturday last, three horses ran away with a wagon to which they were harnessed, belonging to Mr. Jos. Campain and went at a great pace through the Market Place, Bridge Street, the railway gates on the London Road, and were not stopped until they had got a full mile from the High Bridge. Very little damage was done; the turn in Bridge Street was cleverly taken by the leader, and they did not come in contact with anything on the road.

October 1860

PILLAR LETTER BOXES: – It has finally been decided by the Post Office authorities that pillar letter-boxes shall be placed as follows: one near the Railway Station, one at the Victoria Bridge, and one near the Albert Bridge. These sites were pointed out by us some time ago, are certainly the most convenient, and we doubt not that the boxes will afford great accommodation to the inhabitants around each, and will be extensively used not only to their own convenience, but to the dispatch of business at the head office.

November 1860

THE TOLLS: – The toll-gate on the Bourne Road is taken up, and the materials and house were offered by auction last week. The public, strangers as well as rate-payers, can now pass over a considerable extent of good road toll free, both towards Bourne and Deeping.

THE STREETS: – There is an old saying that "comparisons are odious", but in common with many persons in this town we cannot but compare the disorder at present existing in our streets to the order which characterised the latter days at any rate, of the old parish constables, rule. On Sunday nights, especially, the walking ways are next to impassable by reason of their being crowded by impudent, noisy, boys and girls, and the only way for quiet respectable people to go-ahead is to walk in the roadway. We are sure that this matter only wants noticing to be amended.

December 1860

CHRISTMAS BEEF: – The show of beef at Mr. Thos. Inkley's shop during the fortnight ending Saturday last was unprecedented. In that time he slaughtered no less than forty six beasts, all very good, but many of them were of very superior quality. Of course, he sends a great deal of meat to London, but his receipt for last week must have been heavy for home consumption alone. It is understood that his average the year through is rather more than a bullock per day. The show of meat generally in the town last week was good, and the dealers had a good show of game. The Market on Monday was well attended, but geese and poultry were thought to be very dear compared with beef and mutton, and the trade was therefore dull.

THE SOUP KITCHEN: – A trial was made on Saturday of the capabilities of the kitchen, and with a few alterations which experience points out, it will be found all that could be desired. Upwards of 200 poor persons received an allowance of excellent soup.

THE FROST: – However unseasonable the weather may have been all the summer and autumn, we are having a rare old-fashioned winter. On Christmas Eve the frost was very severe, the thermometer marking, at ten o'clock p.m., sixteen degrees only, and on Christmas Day it stood at twenty two degrees, at eleven o'clock a.m. in the shade. Of course there is plenty of skating on the Wash as well as on the River Welland, but the new river is carrying off such a quantity of water from the Wash, that it has not yet succumbed to Jack Frost, neither have the drains generally, in consequence of the quantity of water running rapidly down them. On Christmas Day thousands of skaters were on the Wash and the river, and even larger numbers on Wednesday, when nearly all the shops and places of business were closed for the day. Some races came off near to Batterham's on the Welland, on Wednesday, and others were fixed for Thursday at Crowland, when some fast runners were expected.

SEASONABLE GIFTS: – Besides the annual doles distributed on St. Thomas's Day, which were received by a large number of the destitute, the soup kitchen was open on Saturday last, when the number of recipients was again large, and the soup was pronounced to be of good quality. The inmates of the Union house were regaled on Christmas Day with an old English dinner of roast beef &c., with the addition of beer and tobacco to the men, so necessary to the thorough happiness and comfort of the English labourer.

January 1861

GAS EXPLOSION: – A terrific explosion of gas took place in the shop of Mr. Johnson, tailor, in the Abbey Yard, on Wednesday evening. The cause appears to be rather unaccountable, for it is stated, that the gas was turned off at the main, and Mr. Johnson was in the act of filling up the meter, which had been out of use for some days in consequence of the frost; it is supposed that an escape had taken place from the main pipe, and a lighted candle was used to afford a light in filling up the meter, and hence the explosion. The shop front was blown out entirely, the roof and stone copping a good deal damaged, but no injury happened to the inmates.

SHORT WEIGHT: – Several lumps of butter were seized at this market on Tuesday last, being under a pound weight. It is said that some of it was bought by dealers at Holbeach market on the previous Thursday, and being offered here on Tuesday, was found deficient.

FALL OF RAIN IN 1860: – According to the rain guage at the Pode Hole drainage engine, the depth of rain which fell last year amounted to 30 inches; the average for the last 32 years being 26 inches. The wettest seasons in that period were 1830, 1831, and 1848, when the rain fall was over 34 inches in each year.

The River to High Bridge

More Aspects of Spalding

There is no doubt that in Spalding's early days the River Welland was an essential life-line with the outside world. Much of the land south of the town, and some to the north and west was undrained, and consequently much of the year it made travel and moving about difficult. Nevertheless transportation via the river had its difficulties. The river being tidal restricted the passage of vessels to only moving when the tide was in. Besides this the river silted up frequently thus putting a limit of the size of ships that could enter the port. In later times when the boats became larger, if they were too large to come as far as the town, they would be met by barges at Boston Scalp and the loads transferred. The barges having a shallow draught found it easier to come up the river, very often being pulled by horses, or if the wind was in the right direction sails could be used.

In this photograph taken from a watercolour painting by Hilkiah Burgess in 1830 we can see the view from the Marsh Road side of the river. On the river can be seen a vessel going down stream under sail, whilst on the opposite bank can be seen a man on a horse with a rope attached towing a boat upstream.

The large mill in the centre of the picture was erected in 1788 and demolished in 1909. During the Mill's history it was known locally from the names of successive owners, as Lowden's Mill, Rose's Mill and Barker's Mill. In the background can be seen the Post Mill that stood near to where Fulney Church now stands. This mill was demolished in 1915 and it is thought that a mill had stood on this site for almost 400 years.

Looking downstream from Holbeach Road in February 1922 when this photograph was taken. The river is very twisty, and would not have been very easy for shipping to navigate. There is no proper road on the opposite bank, and you will notice that there are no buildings or factories. It was not until 1926 that any attempt was made to build a proper road along what we now know as Marsh Road.

Planning permission was granted in 1926 to build a sugar factory about one mile further downstream, and this made an access road necessary.

The West Elloe Bridge and the Sugar Beet Factory

The first road bridge to cross the river at this point opened to traffic in 1928. It was built to serve traffic that would be going to the Spalding Sugar Beet Factory that was in the course of erection by the Anglo-Scottish Beet Sugar Corporation Ltd., and this was the first to be built in Lincolnshire.

The Spalding factory was built north of the town, between the River Welland and the Vernatt's Drain. The Spalding Urban District Council had offered the Company a short list of sites, and agreed to provide public services to the factory, including the construction of West Elloe Bridge, and West Elloe Avenue, thus providing a northern by-pass of the town. Marsh Road was also built along the river bank allowing access to the new factory for traffic. These improvements enabled the beet to be delivered to the factory from areas north and east of Spalding without passing through the town.

The West Elloe Lift Bridge

West Elloe Avenue soon after the road was built. The construction of this road then made available some very good building plots, and here we see some of the first houses that were built.

The River to High Bridge

The proposition for the New Bridge and Road came before the Holland County Council on 27th April 1925. At this meeting it was resolved that the County Council apply to the Ministry of Health for their consent to borrow money for the various works amongst which was £13,097 for the New Bridge and Road.

From H.C.C. Minutes 26th July 1926.
Loan £13,536 – Spalding New By-Pass Road and Bridge: – Proposed by Councillor Deal, seconded by Councillor T. W. Banks, and resolved that the portion of the resolution on page 84 of the Council Minutes dated 27th April, 1925, relating to the borrowing of £13,097, be rescinded, and in substitution therefore that application be made to the Ministry of Health for consent to the borrowing of £13,536 for the like purpose, and that upon such sanction being obtained negotiations with public authorities or other persons be entered into for the borrowing by instalments or otherwise as and when required of the said sum of £13,536 at the lowest rate of interest obtainable by equal half-yearly instalments and extending over a period of years, and also the Chairman of the County Council is hereby authorised to affix the seal of the County Council to the Mortgage Deed or Deeds for securing the repayment of the said sum of £13,536 and that the Treasurer out of such monies pay to the respective contractors and others the amounts entitled to be due in respect of the purpose for which the loan is raised.

At the H.C.C. meeting on the 13th April 1927 the County Surveyor reported that the work on the foundations and abutments on the eastern side (Holbeach Main Road Side) had been completed as far as possible until the steel work was erected, also that the work was proceeding as satisfactory as could be expected under the circumstances.

From H.C.C. Minutes 20th March 20th, 1928.
West Elloe Bridge, Spalding: – Reported that the Spalding Urban District Council by letter dated 8th March, 1928, had signified their approval to the naming of the new bridge over the River Welland as follows – "West Elloe Bridge".

When the bridge was opened in 1928 the plaque on the structure gave the following information:–

West Elloe Bridge
built by
Holland County Council
and Spalding Urban District Council, 1928.
W. M. A. Rogerson, County Surveyor.

Constructed and Erected
by the
Horseley Bridge & Engineering Co. Ltd.
Tipton, Staffs.
for the
Mitchell Conveyor and Transporter Co. Ltd., 1928.

Although the bridge was completed there was still more expense to be met as the H.C.C. minutes of 9th January 1929 tell:–
H.C.C. Minutes 9th January 1929.
Estimated cost for repainting West Elloe Bridge, Spalding £250.
West Elloe Bridge, Spalding – Loan: £2,100. Resolved that this Committee recommends the Finance Committee to authorise the borrowing of the sum of £2,100, being the council's share of the additional amount required to meet the cost of constructing this bridge.
West Elloe Swing Bridge: – The question of insuring this bridge, the Power House, and electrical machinery against fire; also the County Council against third party risks was considered when the County

Surveyor reported that to take out a policy against fire for £5,000 the cost would be about £3.10s.0d, and for third party to cover any one accident up to £1,000 – £6.5s.0d per annum. Resolved that this expenditure be agreed to.

At the H.C.C. meeting on 6th August, 1929, the County Surveyor reported that seven tenders had been received for the painting of this bridge, the lowest being that of Messrs. Emery & Co., Birmingham, which amounted to £90 and it was resolved that the tender be accepted.

In the early days the new bridge also had its problems as the H.C.C. minutes of 2nd October, 1929 tell:–

H.C.C. Minutes, 2nd October, 1929:–

West Elloe Bridge: – Damage to Messrs. Birch & Bulmers Boat S/S "Agriculture". The County Surveyor reported certain damage done to the masts and rigging of Messrs. Birch & Sons Ltd. boat S/S Agriculture through West Elloe Bridge failing to open to its fullest extent on the 4th September, 1929 at 8.30 a.m. The County Surveyor also reported that there was a slight defect in the electrical apparatus which opens the bridge which was the cause of the accident and had now been made good, also that the matter had been referred to the Royal Insurance Co. who no doubt would effect a settlement with the owners. The amount of Messrs. Birch's claim being £44.15s.0d. Resolved that the County Surveyor's action be approved.

The original West Elloe bridge was demolished some years ago when the present two bridges were built forming a roundabout to assist the flow of the much increased traffic. The Sugar Factory that the original bridge was built for closed down in September 1994 and was demolished over the following two years.

In more recent times Messrs Smedley's built a canning factory along the Marsh Road, and here we see it about 1970. This factory was eventually demolished and a more modern building replaced the old complex.

Upstream from where the West Elloe Bridge was built stood the slipway and boatyard of the Pannell family whose business thrived on this site for 120 years. The last of the boat builders, Joseph Pannell died in 1942. Today the site where the boatyard stood on the side of the river is grassed, and planted with shrubs.

Boat Building and Repairing on the Welland

In the early years of the 19th century the River Welland had a flourishing shipping trade, there then being, of course, no railway to the town, and the greater part of the inwards and outwards carrying of goods was done by numerous brigs, ketches, sloops and lighters. At that time it was not unusual for as many as forty such small vessels to be counted in the river at one time between Fosdyke Bridge, and the High Bridge at Spalding.

The lack of proper facilities for the repairs to craft became a matter of concern amongst the captains and owners of vessels. Mr. John Pannell who was occupier of the "Jolly Crispin" public house, that was situated on the side of the river, applied for permission of the River Welland Trustees to build a slipway in the yard of his establishment.

The following is an extract from the Trustees' Minutes:–

Town Hall, Spalding.
Monday, 17th April, 1837.

The general annual meeting of the trustees of the Outfall of the River Welland, holden pursuant to the advertisement.

Present:
Rev. Wm. Moore, D.D., in the chair.
Theos. F. Johnson, Esq.
Henry Hawkes, Esq.
Rev. W. Wayet.
Mr. Smith.
Mr. Farr.
Mr. Goodale.
Mr. C. Green, Jnr.
Mr. Calthrop.
Mr. Frankish.

Received a memorial from the owners and captains of the vessels trading up the River Welland, praying the Trustees would grant to John Pannell permission to lay down a slip in the River Welland bank, for hauling up vessels for the purpose of repair.

Resolved that the desired permission be granted upon such terms as the Clerk shall think advisable, and that the slip be laid down, under the superintendence of the Harbour Master.

Signed: Chas. Bonner, Clerk.

The slip was duly laid down by Mr. John Pannell, and he carried on working until his death in 1843, his son, Ellis Pannell succeeding him until his death in 1888. Mr. Joseph E. Pannell who had assisted his brother, but who had gone to Boston for further experience returned to take up the reins.

As in all trades, success in a business brings competition, and some years after the first slip was built, permission to lay a further one was given to Mr. Smith Dring who owned an adjoining yard. This business also did well, chiefly in the repair of lighters, of which there were quite a number trading up the river as far as Stamford, and also to the Peakirk gravel pits to bring to the town gravel for road repairs.

Decay with the river trade led to a rapid decline in the ship repair business. There were several causes for this decline, first of which was the coming of the railway. Then came the introduction of iron for ship building. The late Mr. G. F. Birch saw its possibilities, and introduced steel built vessels, and lighters for the carrying of corn, hay straw, etc., it being found that on the same draught of water much larger cargoes could be carried. Thus there was no further demand for wooden vessels. The third cause for the decline was the coming of motor lorries that could deliver goods right to the customer's door.

The River to High Bridge

When the new West Elloe road bridge was built Mr. Pannell's slipway was rendered useless as it was too close to the bridge.

Joseph Pannell still continued building "Duck Punts" or "Shouts" as they were locally called. These had always been a useful side line for the boat building yards. These boats were used by wildfowlers on both the inland waters of the Cowbit Wash, and the tidal waters of the Fosdyke Wash and the Marshes. For the tidal waters a stronger boat was built as these had to often withstand far rougher conditions than those on the inland waters.

Joseph Pannell died in 1942, aged 78, thus ending over a hundred years of the Pannell family building and repairing boats on the Welland.

A "Shout" in use on Cowbit Wash. This is the type of small boat that Joseph Pannell would have made.

Further upstream from the boatyard was the Gas Works Wharf. Years ago this piece of the river was always busy with the unloading of coal to supply the works for the manufacture of gas, and quite a few men would have been employed in the manual unloading of the vessels. The river at this point was not very wide, and there was often congestion with boats trying to pass up and down stream. Along both banks were rows of small cottages, many of them occupied by men working on the river, and poverty in this area was rife.

153

The river at the Gas Works Wharf, congested with vessels of various sizes. In the background can be seen the row of cottages that once stood on the river side.

Unloading at the Gas Works Wharf

Mariners (Sloop and Boat Masters) residing in Spalding in 1842

Booth, John, Holbeach Road.
Boyce, John, Holbeach Road.
Burton, William, Albion Street.
Clark, James, Holbeach Road.
Culpin, Richard, Double Street.
Draper, Thomas, Albion Street.
Hayes, John, Holbeach Road.
Johnson, John, Holbeach Road.
Johnson, Richard, Holbeach Road.
Kirk, John, Holbeach Road.
Pear, John, Holbeach Road.
Perch, John, Marsh Lane.
Platt, Samuel, Marsh Lane.
Seymour, John, Holbeach Road.
Smith, Arden, Holbeach Road.
Smith, Thomas, Winsover Road.
Tupman, James, Albion Street.
Ward, Benjamin, Holbeach Road.
White, John & William, Holbeach Road.
Wilson, Benjamin, Holbeach Road.
Wilkinson, Chas. & Rd., Holbeach Road.

Crane unloading at the Gas Works Wharf.
On the left behind the traction engine can be seen the Gas Works.

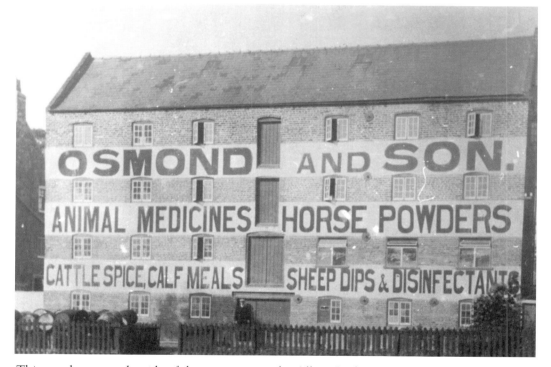

This warehouse on the side of the river near to the Albert Bridge was occupied by Osmond and Son who traded in animal medicines. After the Second World War this building became the head office to the Geest organisation, and carried on as that until the late 1990s. At the beginning of the year 2001 the building is awaiting conversion into living accommodation.

The Albert Bridge which could swing to one side to allow shipping to pass was built in 1844 at a cost of £300 to replace an earlier bridge that was named Chain Bridge. This earlier bridge was so named, because it had a double drawbridge that lifted on chains, and was known to have been in use in 1732. The present bridge close to this point is a single span concrete structure.

Close to the Albert Bridge, and this is the view looking downstream in February 1922. The building on the left is the factory of Lee & Green Ltd., manufacturers of Aerated Waters. This building was built in 1824, and was the property of John Richard Carter who built it as a brewery. He sold it in 1846 to Henry Bugg, the brewer of Cowbit Road. When Henry Bugg finished with the building it became a guano store, and was purchased by Lee & Green in 1890.

View of High Bridge looking upstream in February 1922. The building on the right was the shop of Berrills, and the High Bridge had two fine gas lights on the middle each side.

Berrills Ltd. shortly before it was demolished in 1977. The white building on the right of the picture with a bay window overlooking the river was the Ram Skin Inn that was demolished at the same time as Berrills. This was a very old inn, and was recorded in the memorandums of Thomas Hawkes in 1792.

High Bridge

It is thought that the Romans were the first people to build a bridge over the Welland at Spalding to carry their main road over the river. In a Commission sent by Edward II in 1324 it was stated that the bridge at Spalding was broken and ought to be repaired and charged to the town. The bridge was again mentioned in 1642 and said to be in a bad state of repair. In the Deeping Fen Act of 1661 the Adventurers were required to forthwith build a new bridge over the river at Spalding of lime and stone. As to whether any stone was used must be doubted, because in the engraving of High Bridge that was executed by Hilkiah Burgess in 1823 it clearly shows a bridge constructed of timber, and knowing Mr. Burgess's commitment to accurate detail it can only be concluded that the structure was of timber as illustrated.

High Bridge from the engraving by Hilkiah Burgess, 1823.

By 1837 the bridge was in a very dangerous state, and it was decided by the Adventurers of Deeping Fen who were responsible for its maintenance to build a new stone bridge. The foundation stone was laid on Queen Victoria's Coronation Day the 28th June, 1838, and up to the time of writing this, the bridge is still carrying the town's traffic. Bearing in mind that when this bridge was built the heaviest traffic would have been horse drawn wagons, and the designers could never have imagined the size of vehicles we have today, the builders certainly made a very good job of the construction as no weight limit has as yet been placed on traffic.

View from the High Bridge about 1930. The tall double roofed warehouse on the left was Messrs Hallam
& Blackbourn's who traded from this building as wholesale grocers. This warehouse was named the
"Ship Warehouse", because of the sailing ship weather vane that was mounted on the roof. When this
warehouse was demolished in the late 1960s the weather vane was saved, and is now mounted on the
roof of the Spalding Gentlemen's Society in Broad Street.

Looking downstream at Spalding High Bridge in May 1922. The tide is in, and on the right can be seen the shop of
Messrs. Johnson, Ironmongers. This very narrow building stood on the side of the river, and looking at the site today
it is amazing that a shop ever stood there. The shop was demolished some years ago allowing the road to be widened.

High Bridge about 1900.

It should be remembered that up until 1815 the High Bridge at Spalding was the only road bridge over the River Welland between the sea and Deeping Gate where the three arched bridge was built in 1651. In 1815 the first bridge was opened over the Welland at Fosdyke, but it was not until 1895 that a bridge was placed over the river at Little London. The bridge at West Elloe Avenue was the last of the road bridges to cross the Welland at Spalding in 1928.

The
Spalding
Shipwreck
Society

   "The Spalding Society for Mutual Relief in Case of Shipwreck', or as it is known locally, 'The Spalding Shipwreck Society', is a reminder of the days when the town of Spalding was a thriving port. For hundreds of years the River Welland, which was navigable from Spalding to the sea, provided a life-line for the transport of coal and goods into the area; and also the means of sending produce and other goods out of Spalding to other ports in this country, and abroad. At times the Welland would silt up, and then larger ships would unload on to smaller vessels, which in turn would continue the voyage up river to Spalding. In the early part of the 19th century vessels of 50 to 60 tons could get up river as far as Spalding. Records show that in 1829, 250 vessels brought goods into the port and 143 exported out of Spalding. By 1833 the numbers had increased, and there were 462 vessels in and 282 carried goods out of the port. With the coming of the railway to Spalding in 1848 the river trade began to decrease, and with improvements to the Watercourse larger vessels were able to come up river to the town. In 1892 sloops and barges up to 120 tons could come as far as the town's High Bridge.

Barges around at low tide in the River Welland about 1900.

The Spalding Shipwreck Society

The riverside in these times must have been a hive of Industry with vessels loading and unloading at the various warehouses that lined the river banks. Public Houses were popular with the crews and bargees. Some of these had names associated with the port, e.g. The Barge, Ship Albion, The Crane and The Anchor.

Emblem of the Spalding Shipwreck Society.

The financial security of the sea-farers was a very chancy affair, and it was because of this that the Friendly Societies began to be set up as a means of helping sailors, and their families in times of trouble.

The last two warehouses between High Bridge and Herring Lane, photographed about 1972 shortly before they too were demolished.

163

On the 2nd September, 1844 the "Spalding Society for Mutual Relief in Case of Shipwreck" was formed. This Society was one of 33 similar organisations set up around the coast for the benefit of seafarers. Today the Spalding Shipwreck Society is the only thriving one still in existence out of all those that were started. Applicants for membership of the Society must have reached the age of 16 years, and fall into one of two categories, either Benefit Members or Honorary Members. Benefit Members consist of those who have earned their livelihood from the sea, and Honorary Members are those who have an interest in the Societies wellbeing. A set of 27 rules were set out, and there have been slight amendments, but they are basically the same as when they were drawn up over 150 years ago. Compensation up to a total of £10.00 was paid to any Benefit Member deprived by shipwreck, and should any loss of life occur, the widow qualified for a lifetime pension of 1 shilling per week or a lump sum of £10.00 in full settlement instead. Today this may seem a rather derisory amount, but back in the days when the Shipwreck Society was first formed this sum would make quite a difference to peoples' lives. Unfortunately the earliest Minute Books of the Society are missing, but from 1912 onwards they are complete. Much of the contents of these books are purely of a business nature and not of particular interest to most people, but in the report for the year 1916 being in the middle of the First World War is of more interest:–

The Spalding Shipwreck Society Report for the year 1916

The committee in presenting the 72nd Annual Balance Sheet of this Society for the past year 1916, do so with some pleasure especially at a time when the Great European War has entered its 3rd year, and still raging on both land and sea, also in oceans outside the War Zone, and the most destructive machinery employed to destroy the mercantile Shipping of Great Britain, in which many of our members are employed in, and considering the risk they run by either being blown up by the German submarines or the floating mines laying around our shores, entailing a considerable loss of life to the population employed in navigation of the sea. The committee have only one claim for loss by sinking of a steamer by a German submarine; one death by sinking of a ship in a gale, off the Norfolk coast in the month of February last.

The funds show a decrease of 8 shillings and 10 pence after usual bonus amounting to £10.1s.3d. has been returned off the annual subscriptions paid by Sailor Benefit Members, who have been ten years Members of the Society, also 13s.4d. written off the War Loan. The number of Widows receiving Benefit from the Society's funds during the year are 5; viz: – Four widows received a weekly pension of 1s. per week and one widow took the lump sum of £10 instead of the weekly pension. The usual Christmas Gifts of £10 to the widows in receipt of Pension. The funds invested amount to £1364, together with cash in hand amount to £1400.

The usual Subscriptions and Donations have been made to the various Societies during the past year.

There has been one death during the year, J. B. Binks.

C. Dalrymple Hall – Hon. Secretary.

In 1917 the minute books recorded 4 deaths, J. C. Hack, Tom Scott, Wm. Royce and H. Mountain.

In 1918 there were 2 deaths, Stephen Dunn and Charles Upcraft.

In 1919 the minutes also recorded 2 deaths, William Horton and William Dring.

In 1924 the Society reached its 80th year. There had been one death: Mr John William James, who was lost in the S.S. Rose near Portland in the English Channel. There were 9 widows in receipt of pensions. The usual Christmas Box of £10 was granted to the widows.

Financially the Society has survived, but it was reported that in 1868 with one orphan and eleven widows to support, the annual accounts showed a loss of £10.5s.3d. in spite of 60 Benefit Members subscribing to the funds.

The Spalding Shipwreck Society

In the following year steps were taken to ease the finances and the South Holland Magazine in May 1869 gave the following report:–

Spalding Shipwreck Society:– A literary and musical entertainment was given at the Exchange Hall on the 8th April by amateurs, in aid of the funds of the society. There was a fair attendance though by no means a 'full house'. The various performers went through their parts with great credit, and those present by the warmth of their applause showed how thoroughly they appreciated the effort made to amuse and instruct them. Dr. Morris occupied the chair and in his opening remarks eloquently dwelt upon the perils and dangers of those who 'go down to the sea in great ships' and upon the advantages such a Society conferred on its members.

No record can be found as to how much this event made, but in 1890 the Secretary Mr. Capps reported that the Society's assets amounted to £979 and it had a membership list of 53.

From 1844 when the Society was founded until February 1977 the Ship Albion public house in Albion Street was the Society's Headquarters, and a succession of landlords have been pleased to accommodate the meetings. Some landlords even became members, as was Mr. Thomas Draper who acted as President of the Society in 1850. Benefit member, Robert Hutchinson, married the landlord's daughter Ellen Draper.

The Ship Albion in Albion Street.
Photographed 1950.

More Aspects of Spalding

The Annual Dinner has always been a very popular event, and apart from the War Years, it appears that it has always taken place throughout the history of the Society. Currently the Annual Dinner is held at the Springfields Restaurant as are the Quarterly Meetings and Annual General Meeting. Each meeting is preceded by a sausage supper. In the days when the port was in operation one of the requirements when fixing that date was that "the state of the tide was right', so that those who earned their livelihoods on the water could be home for the great occasion.

The Spalding Free Press of 20th January 1891 reported the annual meeting and supper:–

'Shipwreck Society'. The annual meeting and supper of the Spalding Shipwreck Society was held at the Ship Albion on Friday evening last. Mr. W. W. Copeland occupied the chair and amongst those present were, Mr. J. T. Atton, Mr. W. Stubbs, Mr. E. Caulton, Mr. Grimby, Mr. T. Upton, Mr. T. Stubbs, Mr. E. Richardson, Mr. Gostelow, and a good attendance of sailor members and supporters of the Society. A capital spread was provided for the occasion, and after supper the secretary Mr. C. D. Hall, read the annual report, which showed that the funds of the Society amounted to just over £1,000, £900 of which was invested and £100 in the bank, being a gain this year of over £20. The sailor members numbered 54 being the same number as last year. The number of widows in receipt of pension at the present time is ten. Mr. Samuel Kingston was elected President of the Society for the ensuing year, and the whole of the officers and committee were re-elected. A pleasant social evening was spent, songs were sung by some of the members and visitors, the usual loyal toasts were duly honoured, as were the "Army, Navy and Volunteers", "The Town and Trade of Spalding" and "The Shipping Interests".

Over the years the records of the Society, show many familiar Spalding names. Captain George Levesley was skipper of Mr. Henry Bugg's yacht. Mr. Bugg was the proprietor of the brewery later owned by Messrs. Soames & Co. Ltd., a very wealthy man, whose chief hobby was the sea. They would sail away from Fosdyke to various places on the Continent, where one could buy tobacco and spirits very cheaply, and as Mr. Bugg was a very popular and influential man in these parts, his yacht would not be so carefully examined by the Customs officers as would other craft, and his crew, knowing this, considerably augmented their income in consequence. A note scribbled on a Balance Sheet of 1903 refers to Captain George Levesley as "the grand old man of the Society". His grandson Fred Oliver Levesley was Vice President of the Society in the 1970s.

There were many notorious mariners of the Culpin family, and Richard Culpin followed Richard Culpin one generation after another. The Culpins traded chiefly in pots and hardware, building a warehouse in Double Street to store what their ships had brought from Hull, Newcastle, etc. Mrs. Culpin often went to sea, and was very clever at hiding tobacco, etc., from the prying eyes of the Customs officers by concealing dutiable goods under her crinoline skirt. They did a prosperous trade in the town.

Captain John Gostelow was a popular skipper in these parts, the last of his line as a mariner trading from Spalding. He owned a ship called the 'Mary Jane', and was bringing a cargo of coals from Newcastle to the gas works at Spalding early in 1895, but he never arrived, for his vessel went down with all hands off the Humber. His crew of three were all local lads: Simon Marsh, Linehan and Willcox.

The Royce's were a well-known family of mariners, there being many of that name engaged in our river trade and elsewhere. Tom Royce owned the "Roarer", which he lost; though he and his crew were saved, unfortunately the boat was not insured. He also owned the "Laurel" and "William Royce". Ted Royce had the "Hope", and Captain Turner, Tom Royce's stepbrother had the "Sarah" and "Violet". The death in 1925 of Joseph Royce, retired pilot from Fosdyke Bridge, ended a membership which had its beginnings in the late 1870s.

Tom Dunn owned a ship called the "Elizabeth Ann" and he was notorious for being the most careful skipper sailing from these parts, and if the weather did not look promising he would stay at the mouth of the river till it did.

The Spalding Shipwreck Society

Another Spalding skipper, Captain Walker, had his ship quarantined off Gravesend when taking a cargo to London, because one of his crew had smallpox. He also contracted the malady and died on board.

Mrs. Crookes, the wife of Captain Crookes, went down the river in a small boat with some friends to meet her husband's ship which was due, but the boat was caught in an exceptionally big eagre, near the mouth of the river, which threw Mrs. Crookes out, and she was drowned.

The Hayes family had connections with the Shipwreck Society for many years. John Hayes at his death in 1912, had been a member of over 40 years. Member brothers, Robert Arthur and John William Hayes, owned the steamer "Speedwell" which traded along the east coast until bought by the Admiralty during the First World War and used as part of Hull's boom defences.

One of the last vessels to supply goods to the town was the "Fern" skippered by its Spalding owner, Captain J. C. Atkins. He used to carry maize, cotton cake, wheat and coal which fed the Spalding Gas Works.

We have now reached the 21st century, and the Shipwreck Society is still a thriving organisation. The Welfare State is such that there is not so much need for a society of this type. Nevertheless so many old traditions and organisations have disappeared, but with a membership of over 200 the future looks good for the Spalding Society. Although Spalding is no longer a port; many people in the area still earn their livelihoods on the High Seas. Life on the seas is a lot safer than it was in years gone by, but accidents do still happen. When a Benefit Member dies either by accidental or natural causes their widow still qualifies for the annual Christmas Bonus. Although this is not a large amount it is sufficient for a lady to get herself a little treat, and a reminder that the members of the Society do not forget her.

Members and Honorary Member of the Spalding Shipwreck Society taken in the garden at "Willesby Hall", Spalding, on 14th July, 1950. Top Row: G. S. Kingston, W. H. Gostick, T. L. Mawby, C. E. Short, H. M. Griggs, F. Turner, F. W. J. Bolwell. Middle Row: E. H. Gooch, E. Bain, G. James, J. Strickson, W. Cecil White, J. A. J. Williams, J. Bunting, R. M. Danskin, G. N. Hemfrey. Bottom Row: H. Sketcher, G. Strickson, T. Strickson, R. A. Hayes, T. H. Brown, A. Brown.

Harry Brown and George Strickson. Two old Spalding Seafarers.

Newscutting, January 1895.

Shipwreck Society: – The annual meeting of the Spalding Shipwreck Society was held at the Ship Albion Inn on Friday evening, and being the jubilee of the society a large company assembled, and much interest was shown in the proceedings. The accounts showed a very satisfactory position, and receipts have exceeded the expenses by £31.6s.4d. At the supper Mr. S. Kingston the President, was in the chair. Several of the leading tradesmen in the town were present, and five of the newly elected Urban Councillors, including all the members of the East Ward, and there was also a large number of sailors present. The usual loyal toasts were given by the Chairman, and numerous other toasts of a suitable character followed. Patriotic and other songs were sung. Feeling reference was made by several speakers to the loss of the Mary Jane, with Captain Gostelow and all hands, and it was arranged to hold an adjourned meeting on Friday next to consider the best means of rendering assistance to the widow and family of young children.

Newscutting, December 1905.

From the Will of Mr. Samuel Kingston, Auctioneer who died on the 6th September 1905.
A bequest to each of the ship-wrecked mariners' widows and orphans in receipt of aid from the Spalding Shipwreck Society, £2.

Railways

More Aspects of Spalding

The first permanent public railway to use a steam engine was the Stockton and Darlington which opened on the 27th September 1825. This first engine was the "Locomotion" which was designed and driven by George Stephenson. By 1840 nearly 2,400 miles of track connected London with Birmingham, Manchester, and Brighton.

There were no railways in Lincolnshire until the middle of the 1840s when the Great Northern Railway started to build a line from Peterborough to Spalding, and on to Boston and Lincoln. It was well into the second half of 1847 before work started around Spalding with the construction of a bridge over the South Drove Drain. The Company hoped that this bridge, which was being built of timber would be completed by the end of the year, but problems were met with, and it was not until April 1848 that this bridge was completed. In and around Spalding, 14 houses with a barn and a granary were demolished to make way for the line. The Coach and Horses Inn in Winsover Road was demolished to make way for the road crossing. One mile north of Spalding work was started in February 1848 on the construction of a bridge over the Vernatt's Drain. This proved to be as difficult as the South Drove Drain bridge, because a water tunnel was found to run under the drain parallel with the railway line, and beneath the very line itself. Because of this problem the bridge foundations were weakened, and it was found necessary to add 12 iron girders between 25 and 30 feet in length. A few years later the Vernatt's Railway Bridge had to be replaced with a stronger one of wrought iron built on brick abutments.

Work on the railway around Spalding made great progress and on the 2nd November, 1847 the following report appeared in the Spalding Free Press:–

"We have paid a visit to the works of the Great Northern Railway Company now in progress near this town (Spalding), and are happy to say they are proceeding very rapidly. Nearly 500 men are employed, and the embankment, with the exception of one or two breaks, is completed from Warrington to within a mile of Spalding. "Work was started on the building of the station at Spalding in June 1848. It was designed by John Taylor, of Parliament Street, London. The first station was a very modest affair consisting of house, goods shed, office and a platform. A water tower was built twenty feet tall topped with an iron tank capable of holding fifty tons or more, and a coal yard was sited between the station and the road.

On the 17th October,1848 the railway opened for business, and on that day the first passenger was able to book from Spalding to Peterborough or Boston. The 26th of October was observed as a general holiday at Boston and Spalding in honour of the opening. Five hundred people sat down to a grand banquet at Boston, and a public dinner was held at Spalding Red Lion Hotel. It was not until August, 1850, that a passenger could book from Spalding to King's Cross.

Illustration taken from an engraving in "The Illustrated London News", of 11th November, 1848.

170

Spalding to Kings Lynn

Within four years of the line through Spalding opening a project was mooted for a line to run eastwards through the villages of East Elloe to King's Lynn, and then on to Norwich. An Act of Parliament was obtained in 1853, but it was several years before this, the first of several branch lines from Spalding got underway. One of the largest engineering projects for this line in the Spalding area was the construction of a bridge of wrought iron over the River Welland, close to the Royal Oak public house in Cowbit Road. At this point some of the houses in Salt Box Row in London Road had to be demolished to allow the line to be laid. The Improvement Commissioners tried to persuade the railway company to build a footbridge attached to the side of the single track railway bridge thus giving the residents in the area a short convenient way of crossing the river between London Road and Cowbit Road, but the railway company refused their request.

The first section of this line to open went only as far as Holbeach with Stations at Weston, Moulton and Whaplode. This section opened on the 3rd May 1858. Progress was quite slow, and it was not until the 1st July 1862 that the rest of this line as far as Sutton Bridge went into use. This second section had stations at Fleet, Gedney, and Long Sutton. The line was a single track, and it was operated by the Great Northern Railway Company.

A through connection to Kings Lynn was eventually made on November 1st, 1864 when the Sutton Bridge to Lynn section was opened for use.

Train leaving Spalding on the line to Holbeach.

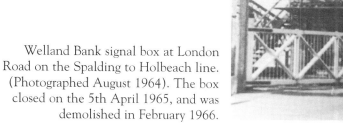

Welland Bank signal box at London Road on the Spalding to Holbeach line. (Photographed August 1964). The box closed on the 5th April 1965, and was demolished in February 1966.

Signal Box and Level Crossing at Clay Lake, (Photographed August 1964). The box closed 5th April 1965, and was demolished in February 1966.

Cunningham's Drove signal box and crossing 1930s.

Train coming into Spalding from Holbeach at Winsover Road crossing. In the photograph can be seen the unusual shaped railway house that once stood next to the Winsover Road crossing. This was demolished on March 4th, 1984.

Goods train on the Holbeach line close to Green Lane Footbridge.

Spalding to Bourne

The next branch line to be built was the Spalding to Bourne. On the 29th July 1862 the Spalding and Bourne Railway Act received Royal Assent. Work on constructing this line started in April 1864, but progress was slow. There were no villages along the route that the line took, so three stations were built for the purpose of catching business from the farms. The first station from Spalding was North Drove, followed by Counter Drain, and the nearest station to Bourne was called Twenty. This branch line opened in August 1866, and was then part of the Midland and Eastern Railway.

The line between Spalding and Bourne suffered as did many more from the lack of business, and on the 28th February, 1959, the last official passenger train ran from Bourne to Spalding. To facilitate the movement of sugar beet the freight line was retained until 1965 when the last railway lines disappeared.

Footbridge over the Spalding to Bourne line in Hawthorn Bank. A fine example of Victorian Railway Architecture. Demolished 1963.

Spalding to March

The Great Northern Railway Co. who operated the railways through Spalding showed no interest in extending towards March. Nevertheless as soon as the Great Eastern Railway Co. expressed a desire to bring a line from March to Spalding, with powers to run over the G.N.R. lines to the coalfields further north, rivalry was sparked between the two companies. Both companies had one thing in mind, this was the very profitable business from the transporting of coal. After much bantering and discussion the G.N.R. scheme was accepted by Parliament, but the G.E.R. had the running powers from March to Spalding.

Remedial work started on the course of the new line in 1863, but it was not until the summer of 1864 that work really got under way. The track was to be a double one, and the major piece of engineering at Spalding was the construction of the bridge over the River Welland, about half a mile south of the Holbeach line bridge, already built some years earlier. The bridge was built of wrought iron, and the overall length of the girders for the construction was 95 feet, being 8 feet high in the centre with the ends rounded. After some agitation from the Improvement Commissioners the railway company agreed to a footway being constructed alongside the railway bridge provided the Commissioners paid half the cost of the additional work. This was eventually agreed. Quite a lot of work had to be done to the signalling system south of the Winsover Road crossing as this junction was becoming very complicated, but eventually the project was completed, and the line between Spalding and March came into use in September 1867.

This line saw much use especially for freight traffic, but with the changing ways of transport, business decreased, and eventually the line closed down on the 27th November, 1982.

The March line crossing of the River Welland at London Road, about 1980.

Spalding to Lincoln via Ruskington

In 1878 after several unsuccessful attempts, agreement was reached for a line from Huntingdon to Doncaster, a section of which was to pass between Spalding and Lincoln. The 24 mile section from Spalding to Ruskington opened on the 6th March 1882, and the other 19 mile section to Pywipe Junction near Lincoln was opened later that year on the 1st August. With the completion of this line it then placed Spalding on a main route between London and the north. This line was operated under a joint agreement between the Great Northern and Great Eastern Railway Companies.

Timetable for the new line between Spalding – Sleaford – and Ruskington. March 1882.

GREAT NORTHERN and GREAT EASTERN JOINT RAILWAY.

OPENING of NEW LINE between SPALDING, SLEAFORD, and RUSKINGTON.

THE New Line between Spalding, Sleaford, and Ruskington will be OPENED for TRAFFIC on MONDAY, MARCH 6th, 1882, and Trains will run as under :–

DOWN TRAINS.	WEEK DAYS.				
	a.m.	a.m.	p.m.	p.m.	p.m.
March ....dep.	7 36	9 50	3 0	5 30	7 45
Guyhirne .... ,,	7 44	9 58	3 8	5 38	..
Murrow.............. ,,	7 52	10 6	3 16	5 46	..
French Drove .... ,,	8 1	10 15	3 25	5 55	..
Postland .... ,,	8 8	10 22	3 32	6 2	8 5
Cowbit .... ,,	8 17	10 31	3 41	6 11	..
Spalding ....arr.	8 27	10 41	3 51	6 21	8 17
Spalding.............dep.	8 35	10 44	3 54	6 24	8 21
Pinchbeck.............. ,,	8 41	10 50	4 0	6 30	8 27
Gosberton.............. ,,	8 49	10 58	4 8	6 38	8 35
Donington-road .... ,,	8 58	11 7	4 17	6 47	8 44
Helpringham .... ,,	9 9	11 18	4 28	6 58	8 55
Sleaford ....arr.	9 20	11 29	4 39	7 9	9 5
Sleaford.............dep.	9 23	11 32	4 42	7 12	9 9
Ruskington ....arr.	9 32	11 41	4 51	7 21	9 18

UP TRAINS.	WEEK DAYS.				
	a.m.	a.m.	a.m.	p.m.	p.m.
Ruskington ....dep.	6 20	7 27	11 22	1 30	6 0
Sleaford ....arr.	6 29	7 36	11 31	1 39	6 9
Sleaford.............dep.	6 32	7 39	11 35	1 42	6 11
Helpringham .... ,,	6 44	7 52	11 48	1 55	6 23
Donington-road .... ,,	6 55	8 3	11 59	2 6	6 34
Gosberton.............. ,,	7 4	8 12	12 8	2 15	6 43
Pinchbeck.............. ,,	7 12	8 20	12 16	2 23	*
Spalding ....arr.	7 19	8 28	12 25	2 31	6 55
Spalding.............dep.	7 21	8 55	12 30	2 34	6 57
Cowbit .... ,,	..	9 3	..	2 42	*
Postland .... ,,	7 33	9 12	*	2 51	*
French Drove .... ,,	..	9 19	*	2 58	*
Murrow.............. ,,	..	9 28	*	3 7	7 25
Guyhirne .... ,,	..	9 36	..	3 15	*
March ....arr.	7 51	9 45	1 5	3 24	7 37

1st, 2d, and 3d Class Passengers are conveyed by all Trains.
*Will call only when required to take up or set down Passengers. Passengers wishing to alight at these Stations must intimate the same to the Guard at the preceding stopping Station.   By ORDER.
   London, March, 1882.

The Bourne to Holbeach Avoiding Line

In the early 1880s control of the line between Spalding and Sutton Bridge was taken over by the newly joined Midland and Great Northern Company. With this new formation much interest was shown in the building of an avoiding line to connect the Bourne line to the Holbeach line without having to enter Spalding station. Several schemes were put forward, and much discussion took place between the railway company and the Improvement Commissioners. Eventually it was decided that the line should run from Cuckoo Junction, along a high level embankment, crossing Hawthorn Bank, and St. Thomas's Road as well as the Peterborough to Spalding line. This also had to cross the Spalding to March line, after which it joined the Spalding to Holbeach line and proceeded along the course of the existing track.

The ruins of Cuckoo Junction signal box, photographed in June 1964. The signal box closed 28th February, 1959 and it was demolished in 1965.

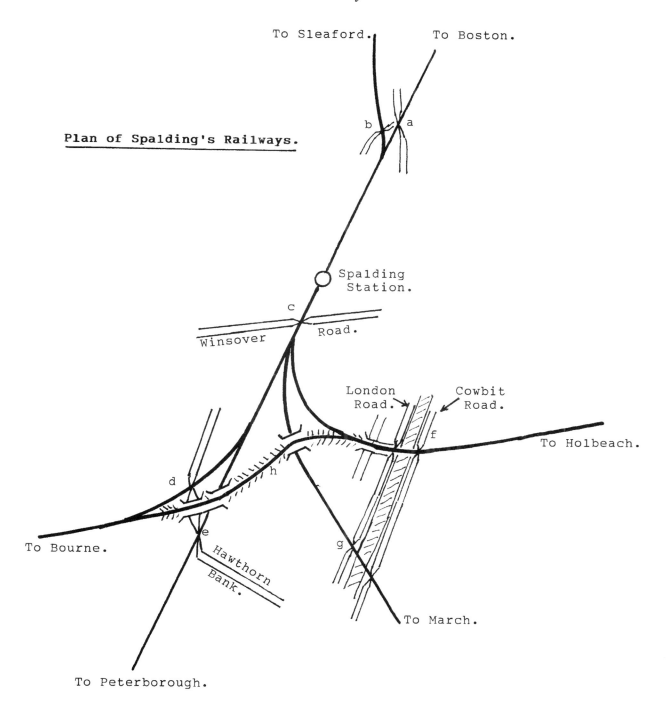

Plan of Spalding's Railways.

To Sleaford.

To Boston.

b

a

Spalding Station.

c

Winsover Road.

London Road.

Cowbit Road.

f

To Holbeach.

d

h

e

To Bourne.

Hawthorn Bank.

g

To March.

To Peterborough.

a.) Pinchbeck Road crossing.
b.) Park Road crossing.
c.) Winsover Road crossing.
d.) Hawthorn Bank crossing of line to Bourne.
e.) Hawthorn Bank crossing of line to Peterborough.
f.) London & Cowbit Road crossings of line to Holbeach.
g.) London & Cowbit Road crossing of line to March.
h.) Avoiding line.

Photograph taken from on top of the avoiding line embankment in 1965. The roadway is Hawthorn Bank, and the line coming from the crossings on the left is the Bourne to Spalding line. The Peterborough to Spalding line can be seen coming from the right of the picture.

View of the avoiding line embankment. The bridge on the left is over Hawthorn Bank and the other bridge is over the Peterborough to Spalding line. In the foreground the tulip fields are where Kensington Drive and its neighbouring roads are now sited.

Railways

As the Holbeach line at Spalding was being widened to a double track it was necessary to replace the single track bridge that crossed the River Welland.

The new bridge was started in August 1894 and the following report appeared in the local newspaper:–

7th October, 1894.

Spalding: – Important Railway Work. – A new bridge for the Midland and Great Northern Railway Companies, built by Messrs. Handyside & Co. of Derby and London, was on Sunday placed in position over the River Welland at Spalding. The structure is of three steel lattice bar girders, with a total span of about 110 feet, and carries a double set of rails. It was removed from its temporary position where it had been erected into its permanent one in five minutes on Sunday, nearly 1500 persons witnessed this feat of great engineering skill. The old bridge was lifted by hydraulic jacks and moved bodily away in seven minutes. The new structure, which weighs over 200 tons, was afterwards tested by two fully-loaded engines, each weighing about 80 tons, and traffic was carried on as usual on Sunday evening. The bridge was designed by Mr. Richard Johnson (a native of Spalding), the chief engineer of the Great Northern Railway Company, and the work was carried out under the supervision of Mr. C. A. Kirby, M.I.C.E., of Boston, the company's resident engineer for Lincolnshire.

Steel lattice bar girder bridge carrying the M. & G.N. line to Holbeach over the River Welland at London Road.

One of the advantages of the new bridge was the footway that was attached to the north side of the structure. Something that the Improvement Commissioners had been requesting for quite a long period of time without success.

At the request of the Improvement Commissioners the old bridge was removed and re-erected as a road bridge over the River Welland at Little London, being a gift to the people of Spalding from the Midland and Great Northern Railway Company. This being the first road bridge to cross the river at this point.

During construction of the avoiding line certain doubts were raised as to whether it was really needed as the following newscutting suggests:–

April 1892.

Spalding: – The New Junction Line. The line connecting the Bourne railway with the Holbeach railway without entering Spalding station is now approaching completion, and for so short a distance in a flat country it has been a stupendous and costly work. A very lofty bank has had to be made, and all the earth brought a distance of about 14 miles; Massive iron girders have been fixed across the roads and other lines; and several lots of land and some houses have had to be bought. Rumours put the total costs at over £60,000! and asks, "What for?" As there was a direct communication between the Bourne and Holbeach lines (as they are locally called) through Spalding station, people wonder why the companies (the Great Northern and Midland) should go to such heavy expense, especially as the new line taps no centre of population and no new district from which any extra traffic at all can be drawn. Of course these remarks apply only to the new junction line at Spalding, and not to the new line from Bourne into Leicestershire. Doubtless, however, the companies have some good and sufficient reason for the outlay, and in due course this will be explained to the shareholders.

The M. & G. N. railway bridge closed and awaiting demolition

Railways

After the new line had been in use for some time the following newscutting tells of a problem that arose:–

Newscutting, October 1896.

The New Railway Bridge: – The line at the London Road crossing of the Holbeach railway having been raised about 6 inches it has been found necessary to take away the strong iron struts or braces which were underneath the cross-beams, as there was not sufficient headway for trucks of hay, straw, and other bulky goods. Extra ties have now been fixed at the top, the work occupying a number of men for many days. After many years of service to the public the M. & G. N. line was closed for passengers on 28th February 1959 though the section between Spalding and Sutton Bridge remained open for goods traffic until 2nd April 1965.

The bridges on the avoiding line were removed in the mid-1960s and the embankment was gradually demolished over the next 35 years.

In November 1972 S. &. G. Boswell, scrap merchants of Clay Lake, Spalding, demolished the iron bridge over the river, and a new footbridge was erected nearby to replace the one that was attached to the railway bridge.

The development of the railway system at Spalding reached its peak by 1900, and for the next fifty years the station and the goods yard was a very thriving business. At the railway's busiest period about two hundred passenger and freight trains passed through the station in a 24 hour period. Because of the several branch lines, the railway complex spread over a considerable area.

The M. & G. N. railway bridge during demolition. November 1972.

View from Winsover Road footbridge looking north towards Spalding station.

View from Winsover Road footbridge looking south with the Holbeach and March lines branching off to the left, and the Peterborough and Bourne lines going ahead. The St. John's Road engine and goods shed was on the right beyond the Green Lane footbridge that is crossing all the lines.

Opposite the front of the station was a large goods yard with a goods shed adjacent to the station.

At St. John's Road there was an engine shed and a goods shed. On the 23rd February 1965 the Lincolnshire Free Press reported the demolition of the St. John's Road engine shed:–

"The old engine shed adjoining St. John's Road, Spalding has vanished like the smoke that generally overhung it. Together with its coaling stage, water tank and engine sidings, and the former Midland Railway goods depot as well. The site has been cleared. The last steam engine clanked out in 1959".

Spalding station in the early 1900s.

View from Stepping Stone Lane footbridge looking towards Spalding station with the No. 4 signal box in the top centre of the photograph. This signal box was demolished in 1922.

Here we see tulips and daffodils being sent away by rail to all parts of the country in the 1930s. "Flower Specials" left Spalding nightly, and in the peak period about 40,000 boxes of flowers were dispatched.

Celery waiting to be loaded at Spalding goods yard.

The Great Northern Railway Co. carriers cart at Spalding. About 1930.

Front of Spalding station about 1900.

The busy goods yard about 1900.

Potatoes being loaded into trucks lined with straw to protect them from the frost. Spalding Goods yard about 1920.

The engine shed at St. John's Road. Demolished 1965.

Footbridges.

As well as the bridge at the station used for passengers getting across the lines in safety to the various platforms, there were three other bridges close by.

To the north of the station was built the Stepping Stone Lane footbridge. In the early days before the bridge this was a very dangerous pedestrian crossing with a gatehouse on the town side. The present bridge was erected in 1881, and a western span added about 1930. In recent years with the decline in traffic two sections have been removed from the western end of this bridge when the bungalows were built in Park Side Crescent.

Also in 1881 a pedestrian footbridge was erected at Winsover Road level crossing. Originally the bridge was built in line with the road, but when the present signal box was erected about 1920 the footbridge had to be rebuilt at an angle to the road so as to make room for the new box. This bridge was found to be in need of major repairs. The railway company decided that for the little that this bridge was used it did not justify the expense of the repairs that were needed, so on a Sunday in January 1985 the bridge was demolished in just twelve hours.

The third footbridge was built over the pedestrian right of way at Green Lane to the south of the Winsover Road crossing. After a certain degree of haggling it was agreed in July 1896 that the M. & G.N. would pay 60% of the cost and the G.N.R. and G.N./G.E. would each pay 20%. The footbridge was opened for public use in September 1897.

Stepping Stone Lane footbridge in the 1930s.

Only three sections now left of the Stepping Stone Lane footbridge. Photographed 2000.

Winsover Road level crossing footbridge in the 1960s.

Green Lane footbridge. Photographed 2000.

Sadly over the last forty years there has been a great decline in the railway system around Spalding with most branch lines closing. As of the year 2000 there still is a passenger service between Spalding, Peterborough and Lincoln giving travellers the chance to link up with the main lines. The goods yard has totally disappeared and Safeways car park now occupies the site.

There is at the moment talk of bringing freight trains back through Spalding, but no decision has to-date been taken.

Spalding Station photographed 1997.

The Railway Bookstall.

For many years W. H. Smith & Son had a bookstall on Spalding Station.
The "Spalding Free Press" of June 16th, 1908 paid tribute to his long service as follows:–

Forty Years at a Railway Bookstall.

There are few better known men in the Spalding District than Mr. John Harris the courteous manager of the Spalding Book Stall, and to all railway travellers who frequent the Spalding Station he has long been a familiar figure.

Mr. Harris comes of a Buckinghamshire family. His period of service with Messrs W. H. Smith & Son aggregates 41 years, and of these four decades, for 37 years he has been manager of the Spalding Bookstall devoting himself to the development of the business with a foresight and enterprise which has won for him not only the goodwill of the firm he has so long and honourably represented, but also the esteem of the residents of the district.

It was in 1871 that Mr. Harris first came to Spalding having previously spent four years at Cambridge. He is one of the oldest Book Stall Managers in Messrs. W. H. Smith & Son's employ, and his record of service is equalled by few. The newspapers a few days ago recorded the retirement of the oldest book stall manager on the Brighton line (Mr. J. Picken) who had been at East Croydon Station for 33 years, but as a record as manager at one station it is surpassed by Mr. Harris's by four years.

Spalding Station with the Bookstall on the opposite platform. About 1900.

Mr. John Harris the manager of W. H. Smith's bookstall. Photograph 1908.

The National School

The National School

The National School which later became the Spalding Parish Church Day School was built in 1845 on a piece of land in Church Street that had been purchased from a Mr. John Cartwright. Mr. William Sharman of Red Lion Street, Spalding was appointed to build the school, which when completed cost about £1,600. Mr. William Granville was appointed the first Master and his wife the Mistress at a salary of one hundred and ten pounds per year.

During the next forty years when Canon Moore was the incumbent of the church the management of the school was almost totally under his control, and hardly any records regarding the running of the school have been kept.

View from the church yard looking across to the National School in the left of the picture. About 1900.

A new Infants Department was added to the school in 1893 at a cost of £650. In 1894 it was reported that 535 children were being educated at the school.

In 1894 Mr. Edward H. Andrew of Great Yarmouth Higher Grade School was appointed by the Managers to fill the position of Headmaster, that had been made vacant by the resignation of Mr. Waring, who had previously held the post. Mr. Andrew took up his duties on Monday, October 22nd, 1894. The West Elloe Magazine in November 1894 reported that, "Mr. Andrew should receive a hearty welcome amongst us, more especially as he is bringing his talents and experience to the district of his birth and family".

In May 1897 The West Elloe Magazine reported the marriage of Mr. Andrew that had taken place on 20th April at Great Yarmouth:–

The National School

National Schools. Marriage of Mr. E. H. Andrew. "On Tuesday, April 20th, at the parish church, Great Yarmouth, by the Rev. S. C. Woods, Edward Hannant Andrew, of Spalding, to Louisa May, only daughter of Mr. Henry Crisp, of Yarmouth." We all congratulate Mr. Andrew heartily and extend a cordial welcome to Mrs. Andrew. An interesting prelude to the above announcement took place in the school the Wednesday before Easter, when the vicar on behalf of himself, the Teachers and Scholars presented Mr. Andrew, with the following gifts as tokens of the esteem with which all regard him:

Oak Tea Table: – The Vicar;

Tea Pot: – Teachers of the National Schools and Miss Mower of Goodfellows School.

Cream Jug and Sugar Bowl: – His Scholars.

Sugar Spoon: – from an old scholar, James Montague Dawson.

The girls and teachers of the National School in 1910.

The National School changed its name to the Spalding Parish Church Day School in the early 1920s soon after Canon Nicholas was appointed Vicar.

In 1930 with the increase in pupil members it was found necessary to alter St. Peter's Church which stood where the Town Hall now stands to accommodate two classrooms for girls.

The boys and teachers of the National School in 1910.

Class of girls at the National School about 1914.

The National School

St. Peter's Church in Priory Road. Built as a Chapel of Ease to the Parish Church in 1875-6. Used as a church hall for many years and also for classrooms for the Church School. Demolished in 1968.

Inside St. Peter's Church before the chairs were replaced with pews in 1901.

Mr. Edward Andrew retired as headmaster of the school after 39 years service in March 1933. His career in teaching had embraced more than fifty years, and he was succeeded as headmaster by his son Mr. Sydney E. Andrew.

By 1951 it was found necessary to make room for another class at St. Peter's by partitioning off another area. At the same time the Church Cote that was situated opposite to St. Peter's was also taken over to accommodate a class. In 1957 work started on building the first stage of a new school in Clay Lake to replace the old one. This expanded in stages until by 1982 the Spalding Parish Church School became a complete unit all based at Clay Lake.

Mr. Sydney E. Andrew retired as headmaster after 36 years service on 31st August 1969.

After the Church Street School was vacated the building was taken over by Ayscoughfee Hall School who used the premises for a number of years before they moved to Welland Hall in London Road. The old school was eventually demolished, and a new house was built on the site. A number of other properties were built on the playground.

Photograph taken at the retirement of Mr. E. H. Andrew from the headmastership of Spalding Parish Church Day School. March 1933. Standing left to right: Miss E. Caistor (Mrs. E. Frost), Mrs. E. Reeve, Mrs. L. Parsons (Lily Munson), Miss E. Wright, Miss Twidle, Miss P. Morley, Miss E. Shaw, Miss E. Simpson, Mr. H. Walker. Sitting left to right: Miss P. A. Andrew (Mrs. H. Walker), Mrs. E. H. Andrew, Mr. S. E. Andrew, Mr E. H. Andrew, Canon B. G. Nicholas, Miss D. P. Ford, Miss E. Loweth.

The Parish Church School building after it was taken over by Ayscoughfee Hall School. Photographed 1988.

Council Works

Council Works.

Housing.

The first Council House scheme was started in 1913 when thirty eight houses were built along Queens Road from the junction with Holbeach Road at a cost of slightly less than £200.

Members of Spalding Urban District Council laying a commemorative stone plaque on the upper wall of one of the Queens Road Council Houses. In the background are some of the builders working on the project.

Work started on the Alexandra Road estate that was built between Love Lane and Stonegate after the First World War. The roads of Alexandra Road, Ayscough Avenue, Johnson Avenue and Bowditch Road were constructed, and new Council houses were built along these roads.

Council Workmen clearing trees to make the ground ready for the building of the houses in Johnson Avenue.

Council Works

Council Workmen with the steam roller that was used to help with the clearing of the ground and moving the large tree trunks.

Taking a break from tree clearing in Alexandra Road.

Alexandra Road soon after its completion.

Before the Second World War an estate of Council Houses was built north of Winsover Road being called Hereward Road. Also created was Edward Road, and First, Second and Third Avenues off Pennygate, The Royce Road estate was built in the 1930s.

On the outskirts of the town along Spalding Common Goodfellows Road was built and also Stennets Avenue, with more houses along the Common itself.

After the Second World War an estate of pre-fabs were constructed in Wygate Road to help ease the desperate shortage of housing.

This was followed by the building off Queens Road of the large number of bungalows for the elderly.

Road Repairs.

Up to the Second World War the repairing of roads was very much a labour intensive job with the need for pick and shovel. The only large piece of machinery that was involved was the steam propelled road roller. These machines were graceful, and often drew the attention of children when they passed by.

Steam Road Roller with the team of workmen.

Road Roller with the tar boiler
alongside.

Council Works

Horse drawn tar boiler in Pinchbeck Road.

Team of Council Workmen repairing the road in Pinchbeck Road. Note the heavy wooden wheelbarrows.

Council Workmen repairing the footpath in Havelock Street.

Street Cleaning.

The cleaning of the streets was another job that was done by hand. It was an everyday sight to see the streets and roads being swept by the roadman with his brush, shovel and wheelbarrow. Years ago there were no mechanical sweepers, and a good road and street cleaner was much appreciated by the public. They took great pride in their work as a clean street was proof of how conscientious the man was.

Sweeping the road in St. Thomas's Road. Early 1900s.

Road Improvements.

Up to the 1950s the entrance to love Lane from Cowbit Road was very narrow. With the increase in the size of lorries, and the volume of traffic it was found necessary to widen this entrance. The local authority purchased the large house on the corner of Love Lane, and demolished the property thus making the entrance to the lane much wider. Some years earlier houses and cottages behind the corner house had been demolished, leaving a triangle of open ground opposite where the Scout Headquarters at Moose Hall now stands.

Photographs showing the corner house that was demolished.

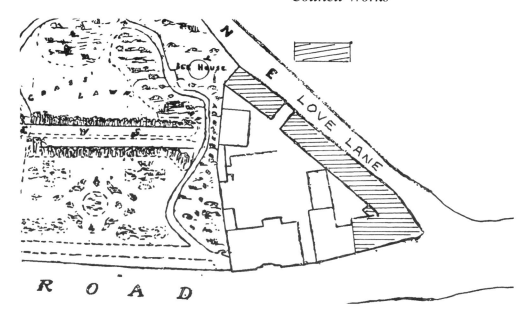

Plan of Love Lane corner. The shaded property was all demolished over a number of years.

View of the corner house from love Lane before it was demolished. On the Side of the house can be seen where other houses that had been demolished earlier had butted up to the property.

Houses and cottages that were
demolished in Love Lane.

Love Lane looking
towards its junction with
Cowbit Road. Showing a
much wider road.
Photographed 2000.

Some Old Houses of the Town

Ayscoughfee Hall and Gardens

Ayscoughfee Hall with its four and a half acres of fine gardens, containing some magnificent yew hedges of great age, is a great asset to the people of Spalding.

Ayscoughfee Hall in the early 1900s.

The Hall and gardens stand as a local memorial of two historic events – the Diamond Jubilee of Queen Victoria (1897) and the Coronation of King Edward VII (1902).

It was as a memorial of the Jubilee of Queen Victoria that the project for the acquisition of the property was brought forward by Mr. Samuel Kingston, J.P., the first Chairman of the Spalding Urban District Council.

The public meeting that was called in May 1897 got a good reception from the people of the town as it was considered that Spalding was in need of a place of public resort such as Ayscoughfee afforded.

Over £1,000 was raised at the onset by public subscriptions, and the remaining £1,100 that was needed to purchase was borrowed upon the personal security of a number of gentlemen of the town.

Further donations were given, and various events raised more money. It was suggested that to commemorate the Coronation of King Edward VII it would be a good idea to try and clear the debt owing to the guarantors.

At a Public Meeting in May 1902 the proposal to try and clear the debts that stood at £450 was put forward. Over £200 was subscribed in the room that night, and the rest was raised by canvassing the general public.

On Coronation Day (August 9th, 1902), the Trustees had the pleasure of handing over the property to the town free of debt.

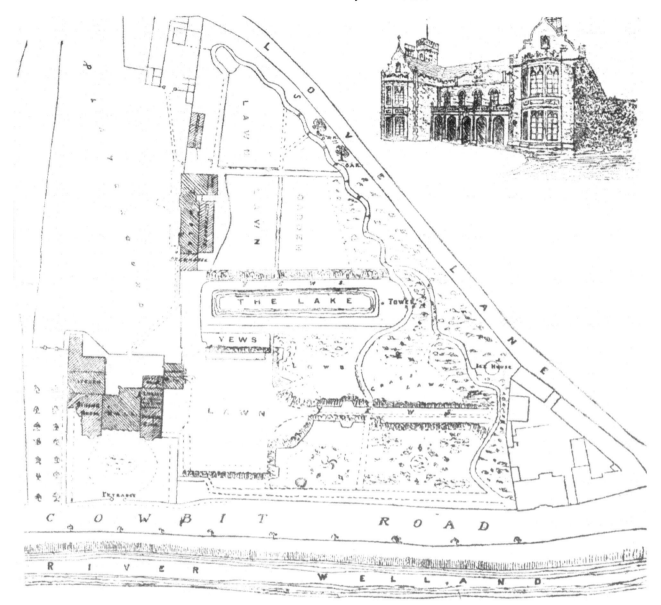

Ayscoughfee Hall and Gardens from a plan. Early 1900s.

The Hall

Ayscoughfee Hall, which is a large brick Mansion in the Tudor style, was built about 1420 by Sir Richard Aldwyn, a wool stapler, whose son (Sir Nicholas Aldwyn) was Lord Mayor of London in the year 1509.

Several generations later the estate was held by the Ayscoughs, a distinguished Lincolnshire family. It is from them that the place takes its name.

In the year 1619, the Hall belonged to Bevil Wimberley, and a member of his family by marriage who also occupied the Hall was John Evington.

Ayscoughfee Hall, about 1900.

Ayscoughfee Hall, 2001.

About the middle of the seventeenth century the estate passed into the hands of the Johnsons, and from thereon until the purchase of the property by the town, members of the Johnson family had, as owners or occupiers, been associated with the estate.

The most famous member of the Johnson family to live in the Hall was Maurice Johnson, the antiquary, and founder of the Spalding Gentlemen's Society. He founded the Society in 1710. His wife was the daughter of Joshua Ambler, by whom he had twenty-six children, of whom it is recorded sixteen sat down together at his table.

Until 1772 the roof of the Hall was thatched, but in that year the thatch was removed and was replaced with slates. Also in that year the Owl Tower was built at the end of the lake. This was demolished in 1922 to make room for the building of the War Memorial.

Some Old Houses of the Town

Ayscoughfee Hall from a watercolour painting by Hilkiah Burgess, 1818. (Spalding Gentlemen's Society Collection).

West View of Ayscoughfee Hall from a watercolour painting by Hilkiah Burgess. There is no date on this painting but it must be after 1845. Comparing this picture with the previous one and it can be seen that the tower has been altered, and the two ornate stone bay windows have been added to the front. These were done in 1845.

The Owl Tower

Rear View of Ayscoughfee from a watercolour painting by Hilkiah Burgess, 1818.

The School

In September 1920 a Kindergarten Class was started in a room in Ayscoughfee Hall by a Miss Henry. The following year (1921) Miss C. L. Johnson hired another room for Preparatory Classes, and took over responsibility for the Kindergarten. In March 1926 Miss Black took over the Ayscoughfee School and it remained under her control until 1958 when she retired at the age of 73. On the retirement of Miss Black a buyer for the school could not be found, so a trust was formed, comprising of local businessmen who between them managed to purchase the school, thus saving it from closing down. Mrs Credland was appointed headmistress.

The 1980s started with the school at Ayscoughfee bulging at the seams with pupils, and after much discussion the Board of Directors of the school managed to purchase the old Parish Church Day School building in Church Street, Mrs Credland stepped down as headmistress, and Mr. Peter Sivil was appointed as headmaster with the extra task of seeing through the move to the new premises in the spring of 1982.

The Museum

Ayscoughfee Hall over the next few years underwent a massive face-lift, during which it was transformed into a museum and Tourist Information Office, housing a fine collection of stuffed British birds, and displays showing items and information from our past.

Inside the gardens at Ayscoughfee in the early 1900s.

Ayscoughfee Hall during the winter of 1900.

Willesby Hall

Willesby Hall was one of the houses in Spalding built of materials from the old priory about 1553. Until the year 1772 the rood was thatched, but in this year the thatch was stripped and the roof was slated.

Willesby Hall from a watercolour painting by Hilkiah Burgess, about 1820. (Spalding Gentlemen's Society Collection).

On the last Friday in March in the year 1858, between five and six o'clock in the morning the inhabitants were aroused by the alarm of fire, and it was immediately ascertained that Willesby Hall then occupied by Mr. Thomas Hilliam, Esq., in Gas Street (now called Albion Street), was enveloped in flames. The engines were brought out for the first time from the new engine-house, and with the river running by the burning premises, a good supply of water was ready at hand, but the fire had obtained so firm a hold that the flames were not subdued until the greater part of the fine old house, built by one of the Willesby family was completely gutted, and a large portion of the furniture was consumed. The fire was supposed to have originated in the drawing room, which was undergoing the process of "airing" in anticipation of the arrival of Mr. Hilliam and his bride. A fire had been left in the grate when the servants went to bed, and it was thought that some articles of furniture caught fire, or that a beam running very near to the chimney ignited, and so communicated with the floor and ceiling above. The fire must have been burning for some time before it was discovered, for the servants had barely time to escape, and very little property was saved.

The house was damaged beyond repair, but was eventually re-erected in its original form, and although having undergone internal modernisation the outer appearance is still very much as it has always been.

Willesby Hall in Albion Street. Photographed in 1972.

Fulney Hall.

After the Dissolution of Spalding Priory several houses in the town were built from the materials that were sold off. The largest of these was Fulney Hall, on the Holbeach Road, said to have been built by Sir Matthew Gamlyn.

A watercolour painting of Fulney Hall, painted in 1847, shows the hall in a dilapidated state with much of the thatch gone, and sections of the roof fallen in.

Soon after 1847 the whole of the building was raised to the ground, and the hall that how stands on the site was built from some of the stone. The present hall being much smaller than the original.

Fulney Hall in 1820 from a watercolour painting by Hilkiah Burgess. (Spalding Gentlemen's Society Collection).

Rear view of Fulney Hall in 1820 from a watercolour painting by Hilkiah Burgess. (Spalding Gentlemen's Society Collection).

Fulney Hall in 1847 showing it to be in a dilapidated state, from a watercolour painting by Hilkiah Burgess. (Spalding Gentlemen's Society Collection).

The present Fulney Hall, situated on the Holbeach Road. Photographed in 1998.

Fulney Farm House (The Vetchery)

Situated one and a half miles from the town in Mallard Road are the remains of a very old house. For some years this was used as offices for the Land Settlement Association, but it has now fallen into disrepair. The building is said to date back to the time of the Priory when it was supposed to have been the Dairy Farm or Vetchery of the Priory. Inside, the lower storey has some curious groined arches supporting the upper storey, that are thought to date back to the Medieval period.

The future of this building, built of brick and stone, is very uncertain, as many do not realise its past importance.

The Vetchery from a watercolour painting by Hilkiah Burgess in 1823. (Spalding Gentlemen's Society Collection).

The Vetchery in a poor state of repair. Photographed in 1998.

The interior of the Vetchery showing the vaulted ceiling about 1930.

Monks House

The history of Monks House is somewhat vague. Standing beside the Bourne Road, about one and a half miles west of Spalding, the Tudor Mansion is now surrounded on three sides by modern housing, but until the 1980s the house stood in its own grounds, with orchards and farm buildings close by.

Monks House about 1900.

It is thought that the granary of Spalding Priory was originally on the site, and was given up to Henry VIII along with Spalding Priory at the dissolution of the monasteries in the 1540s. A man named Kegby was given the job of disposing of the old Priory stone, and it is reported that he built himself this present mansion on the site. A 1574 will of Richard Kegby, yeoman, refers to property purchased from the Queen's Majesty as "my mansion house called Monk's House".

By 1615 it was described as one of the eight highest rated properties in the town.

In the 19th century Monks House was part of the estate of the then Lord Carrington, but in 1920 Mr. E. Smith bought the house together with 91 acres of land for £10,900 in public auction.

Monks House from a watercolour painting by Hilkiah Burgess in 1820. (Spalding Gentlemen's Society Collection).

Rear View of Monks House from a watercolour painting by Hilkiah Burgess in 1820.
(Spalding Gentlemen's Society Collection).

The house must have presented a fine site in its earlier years with a moat on three sides, and the River Westlode flowing past on the fourth. Behind the house were large orchards and fields.

In the 1930s the house had its own tennis courts, and a Monks House tennis club was formed.
Monks House Tennis Club 1938.
President: Mr. B. N. Smith.
Treasurer: Mr. A. R. Turner.
Hon. Secs: Mr. W. C. Bates of 19 St. Thomas's Road; and
Mr. B. J. Smith of Monks House.
On the night of Tuesday the 9th April 1974 Monks House was badly damaged by fire. The house which is listed as a historic building, was undergoing extensive restoration work at the time of the fire – work which included the re-tiling of the roof.

The fire which broke out in the roof destroyed about one third of the rafters, and three bedrooms were completely gutted before the blaze could be brought under control. If it had not been for the upstairs bedrooms having concrete floors the damage would have been a lot worse.

During the summer and autumn of 1974 the repairs and restoration to Monks House went ahead, and when completed the building looked superb. The owners having done their best to preserve as much of the original appearances as possible.

In 1986 Mr. & Mrs. Smith sold monks House, and moved into a new bungalow built in the grounds, calling the new property "Monks Lodge" thus not breaking the connection with Monks House altogether.

The roof and gable ends undergoing repairs and rebuilding after the fire.

Stone window being re-built
after the fire.

This Tudor period fireplace was uncovered after
the fire. It had previously been bricked up.

Abbey Buildings, Priory Road

The Abbey Buildings in Priory Road are a row of cottages that stand behind some of the shops in the Crescent. Before the shops that are now occupied by Bookmark and Bush the Ironmongers were built, the gardens belonging to the Abbey Buildings came right up to the Crescent. The origin of the buildings is uncertain, but it is thought to have been part of the Priory, and could well have been the monks dormitory.

Originally the Abbey Buildings consisted of one large room, but were converted to separate cottages about 1870.

The last time that the roof was thatched was in 1908 when the work was undertaken by Mr. John Scotney of Spalding whose family had been thatchers for many generations.

Some years later when the roof was again in need of repair the thatch was replaced with slates.

The Abbey Buildings about the year 1900 showing the gardens running up to the Crescent.

Front view of Abbey Buildings from a watercolour painting by Hilkiah Burgess about 1820.
(Spalding Gentlemen's Society Collection).

Front view of the Abbey Buildings in 1998.

Rear view of Abbey Buildings from a watercolour painting by Hilkiah Burgess about 1820.
(Spalding Gentlemen's Society Collection).

Rear view of the Abbey Buildings photographed in 1998 from the Town Hall car park.

Leisure
&
Recreation

Football

A hundred years ago football was very popular in Spalding. The Black Swan field (now called the Sir Halley Stewart playing field) was the home of the Spalding United team, as it still is today. Various organisations had their own football teams, and so did several of the business organisations. There was much competition between the Spalding teams as well as teams from other villages and towns.

Spalding Town football team, 1905-06.

Spalding United football club A team. Date unknown.

Spalding United football club team 1930-31.

Didger Lewis

Herbert William Lewis (Didger) 1883-1988.

Born a Spalding man, Didger Lewis was captain of Spalding United Football Club between 1919 and 1928.

He was chosen to play for Norwich City as a professional.

As well as being United Captain, Didger also skippered the Lincolnshire County Team. In this photograph Didger is seen holding the Peterborough Junior Cup which was won by Spalding United 1920-21. They defeated Stamford Town Reserves at Stamford 3-1 in the final.

Spalding Free Press football club, 1906-07.

Even some of the churches had football clubs. This is the Spalding Wesleyans football club.
Date thought to be about 1924.

Cycling

The second half of the 19th century saw a growing interest in the sport of cycling, and in this Spalding was not left behind. By the 1880s a cycling club had been formed, and its first captain was Mr. Stanley Maples. In those days the penny-farthing cycle was quite common, and various competitons were held to test the stamina of the riders and the capabilities of the machines.

The Rev. R. G. Ash, Vicar of St. Paul's Church, Fulney, 1880-1935 was an enthusiastic cyclist for much of his life. About the year 1870 he rode a penny-farthing bicycle to London, and did not get off and walk up the hill at Alconbury whose gradient was much steeper in those days. Mr. Ash encouraged his children to share his enthusiasm, each one of whom rode a 100 miles in a day before reaching the age of 12 years.

Arthur Beales of Spalding was very much a pioneer in cycling, and he made his own A.B. Cyles at his premises in Swan Street, and sold them together with motorcycles from his shop in New Road.

One of the first woman cyclists to appear on the streets of Spalding was Miss Beales. This scandalised some of the village ladies as she rode by, but soon after the critics changed their tune as ladies of the aristocratic families also took up cycling.

The firm of Beales carried on selling bicycles until the 1960s when they closed down.

Richard Wellband of Spalding with his penny-farthing bicycle together with the prizes that he had won. About 1880.

Arthur Beales sitting on his penny-farthing tricycle with his penny-farthing bicycle behind. In the foreground are some of the prizes that he won. About 1880.

A group of Spalding cyclists taken about 1880 on the Black Swan field.

Ballooning

In the last quarter of the 19th century the people of Spalding were introduced to the pastime of ascending into the sky by balloon. These early methods of flying were quite hazardous. The balloons were filled with coal gas that was supplied by pipes from the town's gas main.

An example of the supplying of gas can be read in the Spalding Urban District Council Minutes as follows:–

7th July, 1897: An application for a supply of gas for inflating a balloon on August Bank Holiday received from the Secretary of the Athletics Club Sports was granted on the same terms as last year, and the manager was authorised to purchase the necessary pipes for the purpose.

It was in 1890 that the Athletic Club started to engage the service of balloonists. They were used to draw people to their annual sports show that was held on the Black Swan field by the Spalding Cricket and Athletic Club on August Bank Holiday Mondays.

At the 1894 event a Mr. Charles Baldwin ascended by balloon, and when at the necessary height he descended by parachute giving the assembled crowd a great thrill.

In 1895 Mr. Baldwin returned to give another display, and this time he drifted some distance with the wind, and landed in a field near the cemetery.

Balloon being filled in the 1890s with coal gas in a field at the rear of the Black Swan Hotel.

Team preparing a balloon for an ascent in a field at the rear of the Black Swan Hotel, New Road. Photographed in 1890s.

Twenty years before this in June 1875 a newspaper gave the following report of a Balloon Ascent that was made from the grounds of Ayscoughfee Hall on the day of the Spalding Flower Show, Thursday the 1st of June:–

Rapid Balloon Voyage: Using the occasion the identical balloon from which the unfortunate flying-man de Groof fell, and ascending for his 127th aerial voyage, Mr. Simmons, accompanied by Mr. Mellor Brown, left Spalding at 6.15 p.m. on Thursday the 1st inst., and for more than an hour remained within an altitude of 5,000 feet, and within a distance of six miles from the point of departure. Then, entering the clouds so that he caught merely a momentary glimpse of the earth for nearly the space of another hour, the aeronaut felt satisfied that he was continuing in a northerly course at a considerable distance from the sea, as the supposed sounds of railway trains were heard at three different points, conjectured to be Spalding, Boston and Sleaford, forming nearly an equilateral triangle; he was, however, deceived as to the force and direction of the wind-current above the clouds, for on descending beneath them he discovered that another fifteen minutes would have taken him and his companion out to sea beyond Spurn Point. After getting three or four severe shocks, on what appeared to the aeronaut to be a very open country, he and his companion again trod the turf in the parish of Thoresway, having traversed the distance of 65 miles from over Surfleet in 50 minutes time! Mr. Simmons was somewhat amused by the eager pursuit of the country people during the last two or three miles of his course, and a good deal surprised at the number of them who came in at his descent to volunteer him aid in folding the wet silk of the balloon.

Supermarket in Winfrey Avenue built on the field where the balloons were prepared for ascending in the 1890s.

Picture Gallery

Ladies and children of Spalding knitting socks for the troops during the First World War.

Staff of Spalding Free Press about the year 1920.

Two methods of transport in Swan Street about the year 1910.

Early motor car photographed at the entrance to Fulney House. The car registration number was DO579.

Children dancing around the Maypole in Ayscoughfee Gardens, about 1924.

Pageant on the Grammar School field in St. Thomas's Road. The participants are all dressed up as playing cards.
Thought to be in the 1920s.

St. Mary & St. Nicolas Church Lads Brigade, Spalding. Date unknown but could be about 1920.

Members of the Boys Brigade escorting a Sunday School float in Winsover Road. 1920s.

Catholic procession in Winsover
Road. Early 1900s.

Sunday School parade in Winsover
Road. Early 1900s.

Repairing the river banks in
London Road in 1922.

Broad Street Methodist Sunday School. About 1922.

The Boys and Girls of Spalding Grammar School in 1911. At this time the school also had girl pupils.

London Road about 1930.

London Road about 1938.

Approaching Spalding from the London Road from a watercolour painting by Hilkiah Burgess.
(Spalding Gentleman's Society Collection).

London Road in the early 1900s.

View from London Road with the New Bell Inn on the left, and just beyond High Bridge, Berrill's drapery shop on the side of the river. About 1905.

River Welland about 1920.

More Snippets from what the Papers Used to Say

January 1809

PUBLIC WHIPPING AT SPALDING. At Spalding Sessions on Friday Jan. 20th, 1809, before the Rev. J. Myers, chairman, M. Johnson, the Rev. S. Partridge, and the Rev. J. Dinham. William Rouse was found guilty of stealing seven geese from Robert Randall, of Spalding, and sentenced to be publicly whipped twice and to be imprisoned three months; J. Wilson for stealing some carpenters tools from Jonathan Lake of Crowland, to be whipped and imprisoned for two months; Wm. Wilkinson, and Margaret his wife, were tried for stealing a considerable quantity of wearing apparel from Richard Hargreave, of Moulton, the woman was acquitted; Wilkinson was found guilty, sentenced to two months imprisonment, and to be whipped. The imprisonment of the above persons will be solitary every alternative week.

July 1811

In July 1811, a most shocking accident happened at Spalding. A cow, with a young calf by her side, belonging to Mr Jack Cox, on being driven through the market place, unfortunately tossed a child who was playing against her parents door, and literally dashed her brains out upon the pavement.

From The Bee, newspaper. Friday 19th November 1830

SHIP NEWS – Spalding Nov. 17.
Arrived – Ceto. Pakey, from Selby; Fly, Ward and Triton, Knight, from Goole, all coal laden.

From The Bee. Friday 19th November 1830

DISSOLUTION OF PARTNERSHIP, BREWERY, SPALDING. A dissolution of Partnership having taken place between Henry Bugg the Elder, John Bugg, and Henry Bugg the Younger, (Henry Bugg the Elder retiring from business), all debts owing to the above firm are requested to be paid to John Bugg & Co. forthwith; and all persons who have any claim upon the late firm of Henry Bugg & Sons are desired to forward their accounts in order that they may be discharged.

From The Bee, 3rd December, 1830

SHIP NEWS.
Spalding – Arrived.
Mayflower. Gregory; Industry. Booth: Ann & Elizabeth. Gostelow; and Unity, Bear from Goole; Sovereign, Barker from Stockton; and Thomas & Ann, Bartrup, from Selby; all with coal. Dove, Lowry sen., and Martha, Lowry jnr., from Hull, with good deals &c.
Sailed – Bee, Boyce; Thomas & Jane, Seymour; Triton, Knight; Albion, Ward; John & Maria Jackson; and Good Intent, Barton; from Selby; all with wheat. Industry, Wright, for Goole with potatoes. Wellington, White, with oats; and Jane Smith with flour and oats; both for London.

From The Bee, 14th January, 1831.

SPALDING, JAN. 11. – There was a pretty good supply at market today, and business was very brisk in wheat and oats, each of which advanced 2s. per quarter on last week's prices. There were several samples of barley and beans shown, but very few purchasers.

From The Bee, 8th July, 1831

SPALDING FRIENDLY SOCIETIES. – The different Clubs of Friendly Societies of Spalding held their annual public meeting last Wednesday. At eleven o'clock they marched in order, with colours and music, to church, to hear a sermon by the Rev. Dr. Johnson, which kind office the Rev. Dr. performs gratuitously each year.

After service they paraded the different streets of the town, and then repaired to their respective stations to partake of the good cheer prepared for them by their hosts. In the afternoon they again paraded through the town in a very merry mood, many of them not being in good marching order, yet the utmost decorum and good humour prevailed.

From The Bee, 29th July, 1831

CAUTION – A MAD CAT. – In addition to the many disasters which have lately occurred from the bite of rabid animals, we regret to state that on Tuesday last the cooksmaid in the service of Mrs. Holditch, in Pinchbeck Street, Spalding, was severely bitten in two places on the hand by a mad cat, and a young man named Wm. Rowton, a dealer in rabbits, who endeavoured to destroy the animal, had one of his fingers much lacerated; surgical assistance was immediately procured, the parts cut out, and great hopes are entertained of the patients doing well.

From The Bee, 19th August 1831

THE HARVEST. – The business of the harvest proceeds rapidly in the neighbourhood of Spalding. The crop is good, though there are some complaints of mildew. Labourers were getting 8s. and 9s. per day the latter end of last week, but even this does not satisfy them; several have refused to work for such wages, and have actually spent their time since last Saturday strolling about the streets, or sitting in the beer shops, rather than work for 8s. per day! – Some of them will, no doubt, be applying to the parish for relief by-and-by.

From The Bee, 23rd December, 1831

ACCIDENT. – On Saturday last, a servantman of Mr. Ashton, late landlord of the Cross Keys Inn, at Spalding, was employed to boil some potatoes in a shed adjoining the stables of the Red Lion Inn. The partition between the shed and the stables was only four inches, and the bricks became so heated as to set fire to the straw in the latter place. The fire was quickly discovered, and a good pump and plenty of buckets being at hand, it was subdued before any more mischief was done than the burning of some straw and part of the manger.

From The Bee, 6th April, 1832

ACCIDENT AT SPALDING. – A little boy about 6 or 7 years of age was playing on the deck of a vessel lying in the River Welland, at Spalding, on Saturday last, when he fell into the water and was drawn in by the current, between that and another vessel. A sailor who saw the accident, promptly plunged in after him, and rescued him from a watery grave. On Monday last, Miss Cooley, daughter of Mr. Cooley, tailor of Spalding, went to the river to draw a bucket of water, when she accidentally fell in, and was taken off by the current. She was with some difficulty saved from being drawn under a vessel lying in the river.

From The Bee, 27th April, 1832

SPALDING BAZAAR. – This novel and interesting exhibition occasioned an unusual display of bustle and gaiety at Spalding, in consequence of it being the opening of a bazaar for the first time there. A variety of fancy and other articles, the contribution of friends in aid of the funds of the Pinchbeck Street Chapel was exhibited: the bazaar was attended by most of the respectable inhabitants both in town and country, who expressed themselves highly delighted with the taste and ingenuity displayed on the occasion, and it met with that liberal support it so justly deserved.

From The Bee, 4th May, 1832

SPALDING. – Last week the decayed wooden railings along the London Road side of the Welland at High Bridge, Spalding, were taken away for a considerable distance, commencing at the bridge, and workmen employed to substitute iron railings, supported by standards of the same metal, placed on coping of stone. This is a very great improvement, as it not only looks exceedingly neat, but renders the pathway, as far as it goes, perfectly safe, which was not the case before the improvement took place.

From The Bee, 4th May, 1832

ROBBERY. – On Thursday night the 26th ult., the house of Mrs. Randal, sign of the White Horse, Spalding, was broken into, and robbed of two flitches of bacon, some liquors, and other small articles. It may be supposed that the servant forgot to fasten the shutters of the bar window, as they were opened without being damaged, a pane of glass taken out, and the window bolt shot by which the thieves obtained an entrance. The robbers must either be no strangers, or have made minute observations through the day, as they knowingly broke open a cupboard where the liquors were kept. Some coats and frocks, belonging to country people were stolen out of the kitchen of the same house in the course of the evening.

The thieves are not yet discovered.

From The Bee, 11th May, 1832

TROTTING MATCH. – The famous trotting match which was to take place for one mile for 10 sovereigns, between horses belonging to Mr. Smith of Gosberton Fen, and Mr. Ullitt of Spalding Fen, came off, on Tuesday last, on the Cowbit-road, 1 mile from Spalding, when Mr. Smith won by nearly a quarter of the distance.

From The Bee, 11th May, 1832

SPALDING. – Few towns have suffered more inconvenience from want of lighting, than Spalding has done. We are glad to hear that this evil is about to be removed. Some enterprising gentlemen have this week engaged a piece of ground at the river side, near the building called Massey's Folly, on which to erect gas works, for the purpose of lighting the town, on speculation. We wish them success, and hope that the people of Spalding will not be backward in coming forward to encourage them.

October 1847

THE FOUNDRY CHAPEL. – Holbeach Road, Spalding was opened on Sunday, 19th ult. In the afternoon, a sermon was preached by the Rev. J. West, and in the evening one by the Rev. P. Strutt to crowded congregations. This place of worship has been secured mainly by the efforts of Mr. Hughes, who is employed on the Great Northern Railway.

26th July, 1853

BILLSTICKERS AND THE BRIDGE STREET PUMP.
Some of the tradesmen in the locality complain of the bill-stickers using the pump for displaying their bills upon. Do they think the elegance of the structure is destroyed by this practise? If so, they have only to wait until the Improvement Act is put into operation, and then these men of "Paste and Paper" must "Beware of the Pump".

April 1854

A SHARP TRICK AT SPALDING.
On Tuesday, April 11th, 1854, an unknown person stood in Spalding pig market watching the proceedings of Mr. Hickman, of Pinchbeck, who was disposing of a small porket, for which he obtained 38 shillings, and after selling which, he and the purchaser went into the Black Bull Inn for a few minutes. In the meantime the looker-on sold the pig to Mr. Cooke, butcher, of Spalding, for 37 shillings, with which he hastily decamped. The first purchaser, however, claimed the pig, when Mr. Cooke found that he was duped.

8th June, 1858

CHIMNEY SWEEPING. – A determined effort is now being made in Spalding to put down the cruel system of sweeping chimneys by means of climbing boys. Handbills have been distributed to every householder, intimating that an association has been formed in the midland counties for the purpose of enforcing the powers of the bill by which any person compelling or allowing any child or person under 21 years of age to climb a chimney for the purpose of sweeping it, is liable to a penalty of from £5 to £10.

Mr. Joseph Jones of Derby, is the secretary to the association, and on receipt of information of any infringement of the law he will institute proceedings against the party.

21 September 1858

REMOVING THE HORSE FAIR. – The Improvement Commissioners are taking steps for removing the site of the horse fair from the heart of the town, where it is to say the least, an inconvenience, to the Pinchbeck-Road. This part being improved, is considered a much more eligible spot for showing horses than Hall Place, &c., which is paved mostly with granite.

The alteration will take effect at the coming fair, on the 25th inst.

12th October 1858

EARLY CLOSING. – The drapers here have set the laudable example, which we hope other trades will speedily follow, of closing their shops at seven o'clock for the winter evenings, Saturdays excepted, when they will keep open until nine.

2nd November 1858

NARROW ESCAPE. – On Tueday, Mr. White, harbour master, fell into the River Welland, near the Pigeon public house, during the time the tide was flowing, and had not assistance been quickly at hand, he would assuredly have met with a watery grave.

21st October, 1859

ABSCONDED. – A man named Cook, in the employ of Mr. Preston, watchmaker, was sent out last week to clean clocks in the country, and after finishing his work, obtained payment for it, and absconded, taking with him various tools the property of Mr. Preston.

23rd December, 1859

CHRISTMAS CHEER. – The butter market was crowded on Tuesday, and there was an immense show of the finest geese, turkeys, &c., for which great prices were obtained.

Geese made 9½d to 11d per lb., and turkeys from 7s to 13s each; although the supply was so great, the demand almost equalled it, for very few remained unsold towards evening.

August 1860

GREYHOUND INN. – Under the spirited proprietorship of Mr George Harrison, this house is becoming one of the best market houses in the town. Very extensive alterations and additions have been effectively carried out, and the premises now reach from Crackpool Lane to Double Street, with an entrance each way. The opening dinner took place on Thursday, last week and was attended by upwards of fifty of the friends and customers of Mr. Harrison.

5th April, 1861

DRINKING FOUNTAIN. – One beneficial result of the Waterworks now in course of completion here will be that Spalding can, like most towns of note in these days of sanitary progress, have its drinking fountain. A very good design for a public fountain has lately been brought out by Mr. Wm. Brown, architect and surveyor of this town, and his intention is to make it not only a work of public utility, but to erect it by public subscription, so as to form a lasting memorial to the memory of Theophilus Fairfax Johnson, Esq., a man whose good deeds are worthy of an enduring record. The design consists of an Ionic Portico of four columns upon a suitable base, the whole structure being about seventeen feet in height, with a fountain in the centre flowing into three vases and trough below.

25th April, 1861

TROTTING. – On Tuesday evening, Mr. Biggerdike of Bourne, backed a little mare of his to trot from the White Hart Hotel to the tenth mile-stone at Fleet and back within one hour and a half for £10. He drove her in a trap not at all suitable for the work. But the mare won the match with nearly two minutes to spare. She afterwards sold for £35.

8th November, 1861

SPALDING PETTY SESSIONS. – Nov. 5: Before Rev. E. Moore and A. Howard Esq. – Thos. Hoyle, an agricultural labourer, pleaded guilty to a charge of stealing a pocket knife from Mr. G. C. Bennett, of Long Sutton whilst in his shop. The prosecutor hoped that a lenient sentence would be passed. Imprisoned for seven days.

May 1868

THE OLD ABBEY. – In digging for the foundations of a new building at the corner of the Sheep Market, opposite the Sessions House, Spalding, an old stone wall was discovered, having in it a curiously constructed arch, supposed to be a portion of the old abbey. If this supposition be correct, the abbey must have been an immense building, and a prodigious amount of labour must have been expended by our forefathers in erecting their houses of refuge and temples of worship. A portion of the old abbey still standing is a long distance from the wall and arch alluded to, and other portions have been found almost equally remote.

March 1869

DEATH OF A CENTENARIAN. – On Sunday afternoon the remains of widow Sharman who, had she survived until the 11th April next, would have reached the patriarchal age of 102, were interred in Spalding cemetery, in the midst of a large concourse of spectators.

Mrs. Sharman, who was born April 11th, 1767, was married three times, her maiden name being Enderby. Her first husband was named Bradfield, her second Hutchinson, and her third Sharman. She leaves two children, 18 grandchildren, 46 great-grandchildren, and 7 great-great-grandchildren.

April 1869

HIGH TIDE. – An extremely high tide on Monday morning, March 29th, with a strong north east wind caused such a gush of water up the river as to overflow the bank of the Welland in several parts. Many cellars had several feet of water in them, and parts of the Holbeach and Marsh-rails Roads were, during the height of the tide, under water.

May 1869

Spalding was visited by a very heavy thunderstorm on the 10th May which lasted nearly two hours. During the greater portion of the time it rained in torrents, with occasional hail, completely deluging the streets whilst the storm lasted. Cowbit Wash was flooded and considerable damage done to the growing crops and grazing land.

August 1869

SPALDING. – On Sunday, August 22nd, 1869, the Rev. J. R. Humble, with the consent of their parents, baptised fifty-two children of various ages, attending the Church Sunday and National Schools. Upwards of one hundred children, have, within the last three weeks, been brought to the font of the Church of St. Mary and St. Nicolas, whose baptism had been neglected in infancy.

January 1870

CHURCH SUNDAY SCHOOLS. – The Annual treat was given to the children on Wednesday 29th December, 1869, the juveniles numbering 600, including the Day School, the Willesby, the Union, and the Blue Coat Schools met at the Assembly Rooms at 5 o'clock, where an excellent tea was served to them: they then proceeded to the Exchange Hall to witness a Magic Lantern entertainment. Prizes were afterwards distributed to the children of the Church Sunday Schools.

August 1870

THE GHOST. – A report has been circulated that a ghost has been seen in the railway station yard, and numbers of the curious have been down in the shades of the evening to catch a glimpse of the unearthly visitor. Something white was certainly seen, and as certain it was a hoax, although the perpetrator has not been discovered. It would be a subject of great congratulations if the apparition had been the ghost of the present station.

April 1874

STURGEON. – A sturgeon was captured in the Welland near the gas house on Sunday morning last, and was exhibited for sale in the market on Tuesday. This is the third "Royal Fish" caught in our river within the last two or three years, which seems to indicate that this breed of fish is taking a fancy to our coast.

February 1877

SPALDING. – The Independent minister of Spalding, the Rev. Samuel Chisholm, being about to leave, a number of his friends and admirers have entered into a subscription to present him with a testimonial, and the presentation is to take place at the Christian Association on Thursday evening next. Some differences have arisen between the Rev. gentleman and some members of his congregation, which have resulted in the separation. The testemonial is a substantial one, and the presentation meeting is, we hear, likely to be a large and spirited gathering.

The following articles from the Mercury *in 1878, illustrate a farmer's fight against what he considered to be an unjust fine by the magistrate, Rev. W. Moore, J.P.*

April 1877

To the Rev. E. Moore, J.P.
Sir, – £5 and 10s.6d. costs for taking an Alderney Cow in a halter inadvertently with a certificate a few hundred yards, and for a special purpose, is considered monstrous! The principal farmers and graziers yesterday expressed both surprise and indignation, and you will hear more about it by-and-by.
Yours &c., R. Metherell.
Spalding, April 4th, 1877.

April 1877

To the Justices for South Holland, Spalding.
Gentlemen, – Before you demand payment of a fine (£5 10s 6d.) for leading my cow the 320 yards on the highway without a certificate, and of Mr. Mawby his balance of £10,955.8s.6d for moving his twenty oxen 17 miles, also without a certificate, it is only fair to us that you should demand payment of Mr. Tointon of the £40 fine you levied 10 years ago!
Yours obediently,
R. Metherell.

April 1877

CATTLE PLAGUE.
Common Sense – v. Magisterial Decisions.
Mr. Editor, Sir, – To fine one man £5, for moving one animal 320 yards and another 6d. for moving one animal 17 miles (inadvertently done in each case) it is to be wondered at that such decisions should be designated throughout the length and breadth of this great country as monstrous?

Parsons are educated to preach and take care of their flocks, not to connect themselves with the PLAGUEY businss connected with herds!

Yours &c.,

R. Metherell.

May 1877

To Spalding Magistrates
Petty Sessions, May 1. A Richardson, farmer, was fined by you 2s.6d. per head for moving 22 beast from Kesteven into Holland Elloe without a licence, and you at the same time and place, fined W. H. Riddington, of Crowland, 2s.6d. per head for moving four cows without a licence.

Now, will you tell me why you fined me £5 and costs on 3rd April for sending my Alderney to the bull, only 320 yards beyond the 500 yards allowed by law.

The verdict of the graziers (who are specially interested) here is "the return to me of £4. 17s. 6d. or 14 days"!

R. Metherell.

Extract from newscutting 1878.

It was reported in an article that R. Metherell had retired to Brighton, deeming it unwise to remain longer within the jurisdiction of that Body so admirably depicted in FUN and FLOWERY DAYS GONE BY!

February 1879

THE PINCHBECK ROAD TREES. – For many years past we have advocated in these columns the planting of trees along the river banks, and in other vacant places. Trees add much to the appearance of the town, they afford grateful shade in summer, and they promote health. Lately the Improvement Commissioners have shown a laudable desire to adopt the system of tree planting, and we regret to find that a portion of those places along the Pinchbeck Road, about a year ago, have been injured by scoundrels peeling off the bark.

April 1879

THE WESTLODE DRAIN. – The cleaning out of this drain is still going on, and an enormous quantity of sediment has been removed and carted away. The system pursued is to open the drain at short and regular distances, and rebuild the brickwork over the part opened as soon as it and the intervening space (between the openings) has been cleaned out; by this means only a small portion is open at one time. Because the sediment is very black many simple people were in a state of alarm, and predicted wholesale pestilence. The fact is the sediment is almost inodorous and no danger to the public health need be apprehended.

September 1879

CABS IN SPALDING. – The new landlord of a public house in Spalding has started a Clarence Cab for general public hire. It is a very neat turn out. Persons who want to get quickly to any distant part of the town will doubtless find it a convenience. The cab-stand is Hall Place.

June 1880

RED LION HOTEL SALE. – This old established family and commercial hotel was offered by auction, by Messrs. S. & G. Kingston, on Tuesday last. The auctioneers explained that the sole cause of the sale was the desire of the present owner and occupier to retire into private life. The biddings were started at £2,000, and continued with considerable spirit up to £3,400, when the solicitor to the vendor (Mr. H. H. Harvey) declared the reserve at £4,000.

July 1881

SPALDING. – On Friday evening last a fire occurred upon the premises of Mr. Alfred Cole at the Chequers Inn, Station Street. A large crate containing 10 gross of mineral water bottles packed in straw had just arrived by rail and was placed in the yard near the house. From a cause unknown the straw caught fire, and had it not been observed shortly after it ignited, the woodwork of a window close to would have caught fire and considerable damage might have been done. The flames were quickly extinguished, the loss only being about £5. Mr. Cole was insured in the North British and Mercantile Insurance office.

1884 (exact date unknown)

THE PARSONS AGAIN! – Speaking at a Conservative meeting held at Spalding, on Tuesday evening, the Rev. Canon Moore, Vicar of Spalding, in referring to the troubles and difficulties that surrounded the country at the present time, said that the Almighty had always punished nations that had worshipped idols of wood and stone, or individuals, and he was of the opinion that God was now punishing England because a large section of the people for the past few years had idolised and almost worshipped a man who, although at the head of affairs and the Prime Minister, was totally unfit to hold that position.

These remarks were received, as was fitting they should be, with ironical laughter, groans, and hisses.

22nd September, 1885

SHIP ALBION. – This old established and well-known public-house was offered for sale by public auction on Tuesday evening last by Messrs. S. & G. Kingston. The sale took place in the large club room, which was crowded. The property was knocked down to J. G. Calthrop Esq., for £1,010. After the sale the auctioners, at the desire of the landlord, Mr. Thomas Draper, invited the company to remain, and a number of toasts were proposed, recitations given, and songs sung. The health of the host and hostess was received with enthusiasm, showing the esteem in which they are held after having conducted the inn for upwards of 35 years. The company separated about 10 o'clock.

July 1888

SPALDING. – Depression in trade. A Grave Digger's Complaint. An application for relief was made on Monday last to the Guardians of the Poor for Spalding, by Robin Raby, the grave digger. The applicant complained that sufficient work was not forthcoming in his line, he having only earned 1s. 6d. during the previous week.

1891

THE CENSUS. – The returns for Spalding show that the poulation has fallen from 9260 to 9007. The reduction is partly due to the closing of the prison, and the decrease in the inmates at the Union-house. In the Spalding Union district which covers a wide agricultural area, the population has fallen from 22961 to 21726 a reduction of 1235.

January 1892

A HUNDRED YEARS OLD BUSINESS. – On Friday last Mr. Augustus Maples, wine merchant, of Spalding, gave a luncheon to the members of his family, and also a luncheon to his workpeople, in celebration of the centenary of the business. The luncheon was attended by Mrs. Maples, sen., who is approaching 89 years of age. One of the bottles made for and used by the founder of the business was shown to the assembled guests, stamped indelibly in the stoneware, "W. Maples, Spalding, 1792".

April 1892

DEATH OF THE TOWN CRIER. – Saturday last terminated the career of a well known public character, J. B. Naylor, the town crier, the third generation of town criers in Spalding. In the fine engraving of Spalding Market Place by Burgess, executed early in the 19th century, old Naylor in the act of "crying" is a prominent figure. He was succeeded by his son Owen Naylor whose son (the deceased) followed him. Beginning at a very early age as assistant to his father, the lad acquired great strength of voice with clearness of pronounciation, and he was undoubtedly one of the best town criers ever heard. Standing upon the Albert Bridge on one occasion to test his vocal power, every word of his announcement was distinctly heard upon Victoria Bridge nearly three quarters of a mile away! Of late years his health had failed him, his fine voice gave way, and he died on Saturday last at the early age of fifty-two leaving a large family.

Part of the engraving by Hilkiah Burgess of Spalding Market Place 1822, showing Old Naylor the town crier on the right of the picture. In the background can be seen the Town Hall in Hall Place.

May 1894

NIGHTINGALES. – A nightingale has located itself in Spalding. For several nights past it has been heard along the London Road and Cowbit Road, and numbers of inhabitants have listened with much pleasure to its varied and beautiful notes. It is believed that a pair of birds have taken up their abode in the gardens of Welland Hall, and should the spring and summer be fine and warm, the pretty songsters will probably be heard nightly for some months.

July 1894

SPALDING. – Death of Mr. C. M. Pennington. On Saturday one of the oldest and most esteemed of the Spalding tradesmen passed away. For some years Mr. Pennington had been in somewhat failing health, and on Friday he was taken suddenly ill and expired on Saturday evening at the age of 73. He was the founder of the present business of Pennington & Sons., draper, and the owner of the very handsome shop in Hall Place, which is one of the finest in the county. His loss will be greatly felt by a very large circle of friends. The funeral took place on Wednesday afternoon, many of the places of business in the town being closed. The floral tributes placed upon the coffin were of a magnificent character.

August 1894

DEATH OF A "GIANT" AT SPALDING. – At the Spalding Board of Guardians on Monday, it was reported that James Bradshaw, who was known as the Spalding "Giant" had died on Sunday, at the age of 63. After death he measured 6ft. 10 inches, and the coffin in which the body was enclosed was 7ft. 3 inches. He was a native of Spalding, but he had been exhibited in all parts of the country as a giant. For some months he had been an inmate of the Spalding Union-house.

February 1895

SPALDING. – The River Welland at Spalding is blocked with ice, and even with a thaw it will be some time before shipping can be resumed. One vessel has been seriously damaged at Fosdyke, through being jammed in the ice. – An extraordinary ice accident on the River Welland, in Spalding Marsh, has occurred. A young man named Charles Smith, son of a farm foreman in the employ of Mr H. M. Proctor, was on the river, when it gave way, and he went under. He was carried under the ice a distance of some 20 yards, and coming up again at a spot where the ice was weak, he broke through the ice, and help being at hand, the man was rescued in an exhausted condition.

June 1897

QUOITS. – The Albert Quoits Club have beaten the Ancient Briton in their return game by 13 points, and on Friday last at Holbeach the Fulney Workmen's Institute played a draw with Holbeach.

August 1897

SALE OF SPALDING INN. – At Spalding on Monday Messrs Kingston sold by auction a fully licensed inn in Spalding, known as the Ram Skin, with a strip of land adjoining, for £2,130. Messrs. Hole & Co., brewers of Newark were the purchasers.

February 1898

SEQUEL TO A SEDUCTION ACTION. – At Spalding County Court, on Monday, a judgement summons was brought by Alfred Ferns, who lives in London, against William Goodings, labourer, of Spalding, to enforce the payment of £42 damages given in the High Court against the defendant for the seduction of the plaintiff's daughter. His Honour ordered payment by instalments of 3s. a month. At that rate of payment ordered it would be 24 years before the amount was cleared off.

January 1899

THE WESLEYANS' MILLION. – The bold idea of the Wesleyan community to raise a million of money as a century fund is likely to be well supported in Spalding. Nearly £300 has already been promised, and the friends of the movement estimate that £500 will be raised in Spalding circuit.

March 1899

SPALDING. – A Nurse on Wheels. Spalding being an open town more than two miles long, the professional nurse belonging to the Nursing Association is to be provided with a bicycle to enable her to get more quickly to the outlying parts of the town, when her services are required. The association is doing great and good work and deserves support.

March 1899

CHEAP BREAD. – The Board of Guardians, who have the reputation of being supplied with the cheapest bread in England, on Monday accepted a tender from a local baker named H. Smith for a supply of bread at 2¾d per 4lb loaf, and flour at 9d per stone.

April 1899

SALE OF A SPALDING HOTEL. – A valuable freehold licensed estate known as the Red Lion Hotel, situated in the Market Place, Spalding, in the occupation of Mr. W. W. Copeland was on Tuesday evening sold by auction by Messrs. Killingworth and Son, under instruction from the trustees, the sale taking place in order that a trust might be closed. The property was started at £4,000 and at £5,200 was knocked down to Mr. Councillor E. W. Gooch, of Holland House, Spalding. The sale was attended by a very large company. Mr. R. W. Stainland of Boston was the solicitor concerned.

September 1899

The Rev. G. W. Macdonald, Vicar of St. John the Baptist, Spalding, who recently achieved some notoriety by commencing personally to paint his church and schools, has received offers of both paint and money towards the work. One offer which the Vicar has accepted, was of 1 cwt. of paint, whilst another wellwisher forwarded a quantity of varnish. Ten contributions of money have been received. A London Wesleyan is sending two guineas, wrote that although of a different persuasion he was pleased to contribute to such a deserving object. The Vicar's self-imposed task has been interrupted lately owing to the bad weather, but is now being continued.

September 1899

WINDMILLS. – The disappearance of windmills in the district is to be regretted. They employ labour, provided the little farmer and cottager with flour from his own wheat, the labourer with "grist from his gleaned corn", and both with offals for the pig. Besides which they were picturesque objects on the landscape, and always a favourite with artists. Gradually they are disappearing and no new ones are being erected. The "Locks Mill" by far the oldest in Spalding is pulled down and the materials dispersed by the auctioneer's hammer, and the Sutton Bridge Mill seems likely to share the same fate.

January 1904

THE WHITE HORSE INN. – On Tuesday afternoon there came under the hammer Ye Olde White Horse Inn, situate near the High Bridge, which was built in the year 1553 out of the ruins of the old Abbey at Spalding. The inn which has whitewashed walls and a roof of thatch is one of the old historic buildings of Spalding, and a source of great attraction to antiquarians. A crowd gathered in the auction room on Tuesday when the auctioneers Messrs. S. & G. Kingston submitted the property, stating that an offer of £3,000 some time ago had been refused.

The property, however, failed to find a purchaser, the last bid being £1,700.

March 1904

THE ELDORADO POTATO IN THE PULPIT. – The Rev. Thomas Champness, of Joyful News Mission fame, was the principal speaker at a circuit gathering held in the Wesleyan Methodist Church at Spalding on Thursday night, and delivered an address on "The Eldorado Potato, or a new sort," the chair being occupied by Mr. J. D. Blanshard, of Bardney, near Lincoln, a well known potato merchant. In the course of the address, Mr. Champness produced an Eldorado potato, which he announced was worth £100, and after a brief reference to the potato boom went on to draw lessons from the tuber. The congregation was made up chiefly of those engaged in agriculture, and the address was listened to with much interest.

May 1907

THE ANNUAL MAY HIRING FAIR took place at Spalding on Friday, and was largely attended by farm servants and domestics of all descriptions. The wages given were, on the whole, about the same as last year's figures, and experienced men were quickly engaged at the higher wages. Male servants were hired at the following wage:–

Ploughboys, £5 to £8; horsemen, £8 to £10; experienced men £14 to £16; waggoners, £17 to £20; with 8s., 9s. and 10s. in addition, as standing wages, with certain other extras. For females, the rate of wages were as follows: General Servants, £10 to £14; Housemaids, £10 to £15; plain cooks, £16 to £18; and Cook-generals, £14 to £16.

The weather was very favourable, and the usual May Fair attractions were greatly in evidence.

July 1907

STORM. A heavy thunderstorm broke over the Spalding district on Tuesday afternoon. Rain fell in torrents, and there was also a fall of hail, and fruit growers reported damage would be caused to the strawberry and other crops. Owing to the absence of suitable weather the strawberries are not ripening, and fruit growers are making serious complaints. Spalding Market which was in full swing at the time, was greatly interfered with by the storm. There were vivid flashes of lightning and very heavy thunderclaps. A valuable bullock belonging to Mr. F. H. Cooke, of Town End Manor, was killed by lightning. At Cowbit very big hail stones fell.

July 1917

SPALDING AND DISTRICT SHOE-SMITHS decided to increase their charges because of the increased cost of labour and materials, ordinary farm horses were to cost 5s. hackneys 4s. 6d. and ponies 4s. a set.

Epilogue

We owe it to future generations to record present happenings and events. If our forefathers had not done their bit we would not know what happened in years gone by.

To write a book like this you are very much dependant on past records, so it is up to all of us to save information for writers in years to come.